Sole Searching

Tales of a Thames Fisherman

Paul Gilson

 ESTUARYPUBLISHING

First published 2011

Estuary Publishing
www.estuarypublishing.co.uk

A CIP catalogue record for this book is available from the British Library.

ISBN 978-0-9570635-0-1

Cover photographs © Paul Watson

Printed in the United Kingdom by 4edge Ltd, Hockley, Essex

Preface

By Hugh Priestner, retired priest, occasional fisherman and life-long friend.

I HAVE OFTEN STOOD on the deck of Paul Gilson's boat, the *Janeen*, at 2.30 am with a knife in my hand and a basket of Dover soles to be gutted. It is a surreal world lit only by the moon, as the swell slides greasily along the side of the boat. And I have wondered: "Why am I here?"

But for Paul, who lives and breathes his passion for the sea and all it stands for, the question is: "Why would I not be here?" He exudes this enthusiasm and his stories provide a wonderful invitation into his world as the fisherman, hunter, lifeboat man and naturalist. If you own up to any emotional stirrings produced by a whiff of sea air, you can slake your thirst for the sea among these short stories and poems. Paul recounts true events and personal reflections, poignant and humorous, that come from a lifetime on the water. From the comfort of your chair, you can experience this atmospheric world of resourceful men, rough weather and the excitement of catching fish.

You will find honesty and integrity here, because there is no hiding place with the sea. It is not simply a place of work; for Paul the sea is his daily companion, sometimes moody and dangerous, sometimes surrendering its riches and secrets, and the scene of many remarkable events. Paul's eyes and ears have been trained by that daily encounter and by a flotilla of family members, past and present, who have shared their hard-won wisdom. There are tales of manning the Southend lifeboats and battling to save others' lives, encounters with wildlife and an eye for living history. Paul, and others like him, read the signs of sea and sky, developing instincts that are only found in the hunter. He has an ear for the terse and often amusing dialogue that fishermen exchange with one another. But that is not all. Paul is scornful of those who stray onto the water without regard for themselves and others, and of the bureaucratic decisions which have devastated our fishing heritage.

Most of all, Paul views each day as a special opportunity to know more, and is constantly delighted by the surprises that the sea offers.

I dedicate this book to my Dad, my brother Peter, and my best friend Darren.
All left us when they were far too young and are greatly missed.

THANK YOU HEATHER, my dear wife, for your patience while I was writing this book, and for your support even when it has blown for weeks and we have been unable to get to sea and earn money!

My sincere gratitude goes to Jill Goddard and the Thames Estuary Partnership for encouraging me to put my experiences to paper and sharing them with others, which without a doubt set me on the path to writing this book. I wish to add a very special thank you to a great friend, Hugh Priestner, for his generous time spent reading my stories, for his endless encouragement and honest feedback, and for his many kind words in the preface.

Even before we had a title for the book, I was given a brilliant opportunity to speak at "Shorelines" - the world's first ever literary festival of the sea (Southend 2011) - and I thank Rachel Lichtenstein and the arts group Metal for this very enjoyable experience.

And finally, I give much appreciation to Audrey Snee, my publisher, for shoving and pushing me along to make this book happen.

Paul Gilson, December 2011

*The Southend reserve fleet lifeboat: "The Cecil and Lilian Philpott."
Built in 1940, she was one of the 19 lifeboats which took part in the
evacuation of British Forces from Dunkirk.*

*Paul, aged 19, at the helm of a Southend IRB (Inshore
Rescue Boat) on a practice exercise with two of his cousins.*

Foreword

FISHING AND THE sea have been my life: I have been fishing for 42 years and in that time had a great deal of fun as well as hardship. I enjoy telling stories of the many things I have done. I have witnessed many changes in the way we catch fish and been involved in many different escapades in the pursuit of them. I have tried to describe the excitement of opening the cod end of the net and seeing what we have caught. In with our usual catch, there could be a new species of fish, archeological objects, munitions, ancient canon balls, modern bombs and mines, not to mention body parts. It never fails to astonish me what people throw away and what we find on the Thames sea bed. We have caught mammoth teeth, sheep's heads, a human head and other human remains. But it's not all gruesome. We've hauled aboard a few pots and wine urns going back to Roman times, an unopened bottle of Champagne, a piano, a whole aeroplane, a piece of amber, and a bucket of golf balls.

I feel privileged to have been a lifeboat man for 30 years and to be the third generation of the Gilson family to join the service. Yet it was nothing special. Because I grew up with lifeboats, they were just an extension of fishing and ran close in hand. So I was always puzzled when people pulled on a lifeboat jersey and strutted about with self-importance like roosters with their chests stuck out. Still, all lifeboat crew do a hard job and we have seen the RNLI dragged into the 21st century. When I first joined, some of the boats were 50 years old and were still open boats. "Incapable of pulling the skin off a rice pudding," was how my father described the towing power of these old lifeboats. The hulls had stayed the same, with only the engines updated and just a handful had radar even though the technology had been in use for over 20 years. The new "rubber duck" or IRBs came in to service just before I left school, giving my generation so much time and experience with them.

On a Saturday, after my team's game of rugby, we would have the usual match debrief and be enjoying the second pint when someone would ask:

"And what have you done this week?"

I would relate my week: found a mine, saved a couple of kids and caught a nice bit of fish as well. At that time, the importance or interest in what I was doing, and what I was part of, simply did not register with me. The thought of putting my experiences to paper would have horrified me as my handwriting and spelling was, and still is, atrocious. What my English teachers at school would have thought about me writing stories and poetry I can not comprehend and I am sure they would share my disbelief at what has happened. Although because of my total lack of confidence in writing, I first became a storyteller.

I have had some odd but very nice comments after doing talks to different groups, such as at my local library when I was tapped on the shoulder and told: "Excuse me sir would you mind stopping your talk as we are the caretakers and we would like to go home." I had overrun by some margin but no one had stopped me. I did another talk at a local church to a group of older people and when I had finished I asked the Padre how he thought it had gone. "Blessedly marvellous," he said. "Not one of them fell asleep."

I have always liked words; I would read all the lyrics on albums of my favourite bands many times over. The event which turned me from storyteller to writer was a fire in the building adjacent to my yard. The next day I wanted to tell customers we were still open for business, so I wrote a rhyme about fresh fish being served and sold with a rich oily sauce. That is how it started. The blackboard became part of the business - we would list the fish we had to sell, along with my rhymes like: "We have the fish, if you have the dish". Not much really, but over time they started to become more detailed and longer, my customers enjoyed and would comment on them. I had not realised how much interest this had caused until one day I mischievously announced the opening of "The Kraken Season" the following week. The response from my customers and passers-by was unbelievable. They asked: "How much? How do you cook them? What do they look like?" Of course the Kraken is from Greek mythology, a sea monster. But I could see how by telling a story I could hold people's interest. I was also becoming better at speaking, such as at fishing industry meetings, by necessity rather than choice. It was obvious to me that many good people remained silent because they could not speak in public but would sound off in the car park afterwards. I felt it was better to say something than remain quiet, even if it was not as eloquent as I would like. Although, I would always try and make a joke of something or get a smile so that people remembered what I had said.

It was on those lines that I was asked to do a talk at the Trafalgar pub in Greenwich with the Thames Estuary Partnership. There were about 100 people there and we had about 15 minutes each. I was just going to talk about what I did and some of my experiences on the river. I was petrified. When it came to my time to talk I sat on a table with a piece of paper with a few titles of stories on it. I proceeded to go through the stories one by one and the audience was silent. I did not know if I had got them or not. The chairman eventually stopped me saying that we had another speaker before lunch. I had been speaking nearly an hour. The next speaker came to the front, introduced herself and then said: "I can not follow that." She then sat back down and we adjourned for lunch. The Executive Director of Thames Estuary Partnership, Jill Goddard, got me with much cajoling, writing a column in their magazine, so my storytelling took on the written form. Around that time, I was at a dinner party and I related the story of catching a mine and the experience and events that went with it. The person replied: "Paul you should write that down, it's a very good story." I laughed it off as being polite. I was then asked to do the breakfast show on BBC Radio Essex and review the papers. After the third occasion they claimed that they were getting more feedback than from any other guest. Again I thanked them for being polite but they showed me the many e-mails received - there was considerable interest. It became clear that people liked what I was doing and several others said that I should write a book.

Not long after, I was asked to do an interview with a reporter about some developments in the Thames. On completion of our interview the reporter declared that she was fed up with being a reporter and had started to write a book. Not to be outdone, I said I had started to write one myself, just short stories of things I had done. "Could I see a couple?" Audrey asked. I felt she was being polite. After some badgering I indeed sent her some of my early stories. She came back and said we needed to talk. We did indeed talk, what you are about to read is the result of that talk.

I have been privileged to have had a life doing a job that I love; I genuinely look forward to going to work. The things that I have done and been part of have often been unique. I have tried to put my experiences to paper, some funny and some sad. Some of my experiences happened some time ago, but they are as I remember them. I hope you enjoy reading about them as much as I did living them.

Paul, aged 20, on The Anja, with Dad at the helm in the wheelhouse.

Fishing is a Drug

I ALWAYS WANTED TO be a fisherman, as far back as I can remember. One of the first things I would do Dad when he came home from work was to find out who had caught the most. Even if I was in bed, I would call out: "Who was top boat today?"

My wife just says it's in the genes. I am at least sixth-generation fisherman and being a family business, we were taught the old way - by stories. This method has been used by hunters since time began and it worked for me. I was very lucky as a kid; my father was also the lifeboat coxswain as well as a fisherman so it was boats and more boats. Wherever we went on holiday or a day out it was on the coast. Dad was one of seven: he had four brothers and two sisters, all the brothers were fishermen. Grandfather was a fisherman but he was soon usurped by his youngest son who he had as his crew. This was Lawrence, Dad's youngest brother, known to us as Lol. Grandfather came ashore and sold the fish for the Gillies - the family nickname.

Dad's oldest brother was Ray, a great inventor and a very good fisherman. He was in charge of the Admiral's Barge (which was the admiral's personal run-about, used for errands and orders/messages to the ships within his charge.) It was moored at the end of Southend Pier during the war and Ray would be sent fishing by the admiral to top up what I was told were very basic rations. Any chain or wire left lying about would appear as if by magic aboard the launch and was quickly converted into fishing gear. Apparently with two high-powered petrol engines, he would be sent off at speed most evenings. (I have recently learnt that this may not be completely true, and that it was Dad who would take the boat out. If this was the case he would have been only in his teens, but Dad said it was Ray so I will stick with that.) I was always pleased to be going out with Ray and Lol, as we caught lots of fish and worked hard but it was so much fun. They both told good stories, but with Lol you also got bacon sandwiches and great big pieces of ginger cake, with Ray you got to steer the boat. When Ray died, God got another fisherman, but this one had a special sparkle in his eye. Ray had two sons, John and Patrick, who became fishermen. He also had two daughters, Jean and Melanie. Jean became an officer in the Salvation Army and then a social worker. Melanie, well, she was the baby, but she did join the family business later.

The next brother was Bram, or to give him his full name, Bramwell - after General Booth of Salvation Army fame. The whole family were Salvationists. Bram joined the Royal Navy and was drafted into the destroyers as an electrician (which still surprises me to this day). He was also a very good footballer and boxer. The Navy would send him all over the place if there was a game or fight to be had, and he did say that he liked beating the Army the most. Unfortunately Bram paid a heavy price for his love of the sport: he was kicked in the legs so often that in middle age his legs became very ulcerated and this prevented him from going fishing.

Bram also experienced one of the tragedies of war when his ship steamed through survivors from a merchant ship sunk by a submarine. The submarine was under the survivors and they had to depth-charge the area otherwise the sub would have got them too. He went grey over night and his skin became blotchy. This was something that he never talked about and I only got this story from Dad once. It was not to be spoken about again. Still, Bram was great to us kids as well as his two own daughters.

He named his boat *The Little Butch* after his youngest daughter Susan. Saturday mornings Bram would take us all out angling with his crew, a very tall man called Derrick Tyrrell who turned into very good fisherman after Bram went ashore. Fishing alongside them on these angling trips would be as many as eight children, all aged under ten. The competition among us was as strong then as it is today. Derrick left the family firm before I became skipper and became a designer for Matchbox toys, a very nice guy. He did come out with me a few times and it was always a pleasure. He was a very good teacher and I learnt a lot from him.

Bram's eldest daughter Janet was our baby-sitter when our parents went out to a dinner or dance. She would read us stories of gladiators and animals eating the slaves in the arena. We just were not into fairy tales. Janet joined the Salvation Army and became an officer. She worked for many years in Russia and she loved it. Tragically, shortly after her retirement she went to visit her niece who was living in Hong Kong. We do not know what happened yet, but she was murdered in 2011, allegedly by the niece's estranged husband. A terrible end to a truly good woman.

The next brother was Norman. I had problems with Norm and just could not make a friend of him. He was different to the others, possibly because he had a stiff leg after an accident when he was a child. Fortunately I was not alone when it came to being difficult, as almost everyone else had a problem with Norm now and again.

Dad told a story of coming home to Granddad's on a Saturday night after taking a young woman to the pictures. He walked in to meet Granddad behind the front door who promptly punched him to the ground.

"You don't go out with married women" was all he said. This was news to Dad but not to Norman, who had got home earlier and told his father that Peter was taking out a woman who was married to a soldier .

Norman had two daughters (Norma and Alison) and sons Bill and Glyn who joined the family firm and now operate the two boats near the pier. They must be the most photographed fishing boats in the world. An odd thing, both Bill and Glyn have birthdays only five days apart from my brother and I - must have been windy days and our dads all went home early.

The next of the family to come along was Doreen. She was a seamstress and did not marry until late in life. She was very good to us when we were kids, taking us out often in her soft top Morris Minor.

Then came my dad, Peter. We did not always see eye to eye once I became a teenager. Possibly because I played rugby and not the family game of football - he spent hours teaching me to kick with both feet, only to see me pick the ball up and run with it. It was his fault though; he was a smoker and would send me up the road to the corner shop to buy his cigarettes for the next day's fishing. I would take a ball but you could not run flat out kicking a ball so it went under my arm. It stayed there until I was in my forties. Dad was the youngest coxswain of a RNLI lifeboat when he took over just after the 1953 floods. He was away for three days, mostly on Foulness Island; nine months after his return, I turned up.

As I have said, he would tell me stories of fishing and life boats when he put me and my brother to bed - none of these namby-pamby fairy tales or storybooks from him. I have so many of his traits: flat feet, diabetes, a fiery temper, a liking of motorbikes but most of all the love of fishing. Dad died at sea. Smoking got him in the end; he was only 62. He was pair-fishing for sprats with his friend Colin Knapp. On their first haul they had filled the net up. Dad punched the air said: "Yes," and dropped dead. Too young, but he had a net full of fish and with his mates, doing the job he loved.

A better end than poor Colin who suffered with prostate cancer for so long before leaving us.

For the few years we worked together as a team - three boats, two nets and nine men - it was great fun, as you will read later.

That leaves us with Lol, possibly the best fisherman of the family, although they were all good in their day. Dad had a crewman who had escaped from Belgium at the start of the war. His real name I do not know, but we knew him as Belgie Joe. I can just remember Joe as a nice warm man. When I was a toddler he filled a bucket with water and put some fish in it for me to watch. As soon as his back was turned I was in the bucket trying to catch the fish. He called out to Dad: "I think we have a fishermen here."

Hopefully I have not let him down. He settled here and married an English woman and became Dad's crew and friend. Lol would be with Joe making nets before he left school and they would race each other filling needles and emptying them. Lol learnt much from him. I am sure he was certainly the fastest net mender we had but he did get more practice than most. If he felt there were fish about while on the boat, he would have a go and shoot. I remember meeting him in from school one day and the nets he was mending were not that big but he had six of them on the boat and every one was torn or damaged in some way. We had been asked to go and gut the fish while he and his crew - cousin John, Ray's eldest son - tried to put some nets back together for the next day. He had been working in Sheerness Harbour on a very rough piece of ground and had caught many boxes of sole and several lobsters. I learnt years later that a whole ship had blown up there while loading sea mines, killing hundreds of men, leaving no survivors nor any remains of the ship. Joe died young while fishing with Dad, slipping away in his arms.

The only picture we have of Dad's crew Belgie Joe (in foreground).

Lol was a very good footballer, as were all the brothers, but I do remember him still playing, he was the youngest after all. He would take all us youngsters with him on the back of the fish truck to his games and many an adventure was had on those Saturday afternoons.

I have two aunts Doreen and Betty. Doreen was very good with us kids and I spent many happy hours in her company when my parents were visiting my brother in hospital.

The Gilson family on holiday. Paul is standing with his parents.
His brother Peter is in the foreground.

My brother Peter, or little Pete as he was called, was four years younger than me. He never had good health, as I remember. He had kidney failure. Dialysis was in its early stages back then; it was too late to help him. When he was well he was a fantastic comedian with jokes streaming from him and with a laugh that would melt an iceberg. He and Dad were very close as they spent so much time together, out and about in the car with our old Dachshund, Sandy, at every opportunity. Unfortunately he passed away when he was 14 years old, something that Dad never got over.

That leaves my sister Tracy. She was born just before Peter died. Our age difference and my new girlfriend - later wife - took me away from the family home while she grew up.

Fishing is a drug, an obsession, and a threatened way of life. I only ever wanted to catch fish, but I have become a politician, environmentalist, speaker, lifeboat man, a Freeman of Southend and I now get asked to review the papers for the local BBC radio station. Who would have thought it?

Greater London 2 Lifeboat launching at Southend.
Paul, on portside (left), is about to position the rudder.

Call for the Boat

ONE OF MY first memories of Dad on the lifeboat was sitting in our back room watching the telly with Mum. We knew Dad was out in the boat (the lifeboat was only ever referred to as "the boat," i.e. "a call for the boat,") but not much else. He had been away a long time but we were used to him being away. Then, there he was on the news! There was an image of him standing in front of the lifeboat, which was stuck high out of the water with a breakwater plank stuck in her bottom, in very misty conditions. My brother and I were in shock, as we screamed at the telly: "It's Dad. It's Dad!"

We could not hear what was said: we were too excited. When he eventually came home he told us about what happened. They had launched late at night following cries for help at Shoebury West Beach. It was dense fog; they had managed to get to the area with only a compass and echo sounder. The sounder was useless in shallow water so just on Dad's skill he got to the right place. (Years later, I had to do the same thing myself in an inshore rescue boat. It was no mean feat - and to think his boat was 40 feet long). On West Beach there are big breakwaters and two jetties that are used by the Ministry of Defence (MOD). The cries for help were in that area. The bowman on the lifeboat heard the people call out, he pointed and cried: "Over there, Peter."

Dad edged the boat in that direction, but did not know that he was heading straight for one of the jetties.

"Hard astern, give it to her!" the bowman called out.

In the fog and darkness Dad lost his bearings and there was a big crash and bang. She reared up, stopped and despite all his efforts, she would not move. She was stuck. There was nothing they could do, but wait for the tide to go out. The people in trouble had become silent. With daylight, the worst was revealed. The lifeboat was high and dry with two piles through her bottom. Even worse, there were two bodies on the mud only a few hundred yards way.

The two piles were cut off in situ and after pulling her up the slipway back on station she had to go away to be repaired. It took Dad a long time to get over that event, to be so close and yet fail.

I did something similar some 20 years later. We were tasked by the Coastguard to cries for help off Westcliff. I had seen a boat hours earlier when we had come home from sea so I had an idea where to go. It was quite rough, about a force six from the south. There were two of us in the inshore rescue boat. We went as fast as conditions allowed but we were being thrown about, often jumping right out of the water. I tried to go along the shore just outside the breakwaters; we had some 150 metres to go when I heard a scream.

"Did you hear that scream?" I shouted to Clifton, my crew.

"You're dreaming, I only heard seagulls," he replied.

"I am sure it was."

"We've got miles to go yet," he insisted, "let's push on."

Reluctantly I agreed. We could see the Coastguard was on the scene, or to where they thought the cries for help had come from. It was due north of where the boat I had seen earlier was moored. We did a couple of sweeps when we heard a call: "Something on the beach, but back to the east". I knew where I was going: straight back to where I had heard the scream, so straight up the beach we went. We were right next to a very big body just at the water's edge. We jumped out the boat and dragged the man clear of the water. He had lots of clothes on and was very heavy. The ambulance arrived very quickly and everything was done to resuscitate him, but to no avail. I had failed to do what my instincts had told me. I sat on the sea wall, mortified. " If only," kept going through my head: "if only," I cried. As it turned out we would not have been able to save him, after swimming or drifting in, he had suffered a heart attack probably at the foot of the beach. Carrying all that weight had probably been too much for his heart. I have heard that scream many times since, so I know now just how Dad felt.

Some months later, when Dad's lifeboat *Greater London 2* was still under repair, the annual men's dinner for the crews of the Southend Lifeboat was taking place at the Kursaal Dining and Banqueting suite. This was a traditional dinner given by the town's people as a thank you to the crews of the Southend Lifeboat.

They bought tickets and paid a bit more so the crew had a free dinner. Usually a comedian or some other kind of entertainment was laid on. I saw my first stripper at one of these dinners: what a waste of time! However, at this dinner just after the meal, Percy Garon, the Honorary Secretary, stood up and described the call that resulted in the damage to *Greater London 2* and the reasons for her being away so long. He then made a signal to men at the doors all around the hall who locked the doors.

He then said: "Gentlemen, I need £2,200 for a radar. You're not leaving until I have it." I am told it took less that five minutes to get that money, and this was in the Sixties. I wonder how much would that be now? "Thank you," he said once the money was collected. "I knew you would not let us down."

It was a type 17 Kelvin and Hughes radar - indeed a very high quality radar that gave many years of good service.

Another early memory is answering the telephone when Dad was out on "the boat". I would be talking to all the major newspapers and just telling them what the call was. It was odd. My teachers and friends never believed me when I said I had been talking to the Daily Express or Telegraph the previous night.

I also remember collecting up the log sheets and working out the rewards that were to be paid to the crew for the service. I cannot remember the exact amount but a pound and 10 shillings per service up to so many hours and then after that there was a bit more. A pittance, but I do not ever remember any one asking for it - although after the war things were so hard that every penny counted and a ticket was given as you entered the boathouse.

One event that's still as clear and painful as when it happened to me at the age of ten, took place on a Christmas Eve. "The boat" was out and Mum had got the raving hump about it, so she opened a bottle of port and offered me some. It was the first time that alcohol had passed my lips and I have got to say it was good. However, after several of these I remember feeling very tired and wobbly. I crawled up the stairs and fell into bed. I woke the next morning with a hangover I was never to forget. I don't think Dad ever knew what happened that night, but he was there the next time I drank. It was at one of those lifeboat dinners. It was my second dinner and I was now an active crewman. The old hands made it their job to look after me.

"Try this, you'll like this, light and bitter, rum, gin and tonic." Oh they looked after me okay. The next morning I had to go off on the mud to put out a storm anchor, as I lifted the chain up my head nearly exploded. Dad thought this oh so very funny.

I drank pints of Coke for many years after that.

Paul on board the Anja, emptying the cod end.

29 Stone of Sole

I WAS A KEEN teen. Aged 19, I could not wait for dad to go on holiday, as this would give me the opportunity to take his boat the *Anja* to sea on my own. None of my friends knew the boat nor had any knowledge of beam trawling, so it would be me and a crew from another trawler. It was mid-June and Dad duly went away, leaving me with the keys to the boat. The water was clear so we decided it would be night fishing for us. Bob, crew from the *Ros Beara*, and I made orders for 8 pm Sunday evening. Not the nicest time to go to sea, but we knew the best time to go fishing was when the water was clear. I was so excited, I would not have slept anyway.

Anja was moored in the Ray at Old Leigh and we got aboard about 8.45pm after an uneventful ride in the motor boat. I had already made up my mind where we would be fishing and how the night should pan out. We steamed down the river, with great confidence that we were about to empty the sea of fish! However, the weather had other ideas, for as we were outward bound it shut in thick fog. We slowed up and waited around, hoping the fog would clear. This was a real peasouper: that thick it was coming through the wheelhouse window like cold steam. After hanging around for about half an hour, I turned round and headed back to our moorings, but it did not improve and the tide was dropping fast. I was forced by time to head for our second mooring next to Southend Pier on the foreshore. I felt that it would be the easiest mooring to find in the dark and fog. I could follow the pier on the radar and as the mooring was only 50 yards from the pier I would run straight in to it. Well, it was a good plan. The radar on the *Anja* had possibly come from a big ship originally and it was very temperamental, but that day it worked well. I let the side down, trying to steer and watch the radar at the same time. We did not have the luxury of an auto-pilot in those days, which holds the ship on a steady course. Then it was all done by hand. I managed to pass the end of the Boom, but it was very close. The glow from the light illuminated the fog, turning it green. I passed the mid-Shoebury buoy without seeing it, but it did not have a light anyway. The next obstacle was going to be the Mulberry Harbour.[1]

Fortunately, we got past this without any problems, but the tide was dropping fast and my steering was erratic. Thankfully very few boats back then went to sea when it was foggy, unlike modern vessels which can carry on as if it was a nice sunny day. Nowadays, I don't worry about working in dense fog - once we are clear of the quay that's it, we go. We didn't have that luxury that night, so when we again found the end of the pier, we followed it north toward the shore. The tide was getting very low, so I knew we would not have much time to muck about when and if we found the mooring. I could see the *Black Gang* boats[2] on the moorings so I had a good idea where to head for, luck was with me and we could see the odd light on the pier.

As if by magic we found the mooring and we pulled it aboard. The sense of relief was unimaginable. We'd made it. Trouble was, the tide was going out and we had to wait before we tried to get ashore. Once we had stopped the engine, all was silent. We could hear the traffic on the seafront, but nobody would be coming to get us so we would have to wait and walk ashore when the tide went out. After what seemed an age, the boat took the ground and eventually the tide left her. We got over the side and walked toward the pier and then followed that to the shore. It was 1am by the time I got back home. My eyes were popping out of my head and I was exhausted. My bed and new wife were most welcome.

We had made orders for the same time on Monday evening, the fog had cleared and it was a delightful evening. As we made our way off the shore to the deeper water, I could see a set of lights leaving Hadleigh Ray, and thought it might be Colin Knapp on the *Ina K*. She was a beamer like us but with more power. Colin and his son Ken kept her in tip-top condition. She was so spotless an engineer was heard to say that his overalls were cleaner when he finished working on her than when he arrived.

---

[1] *A large piece of war-time wreckage that broke its back while being towed to northern France and ran aground on the eve of D-Day in 1944.*

[2] *The Black Gang were the two smallest boats in the firm. They worked as a team mostly pair-trawling for eels in the summer and whitebait and cod in the winter. They were painted black and were always together, hence the name "Black Gang".*

At that time, Colin was the competition, although still a good friend. We said a quick hello and discussed the fog. The previous night, he had turned out later than us and was just about to leave Leigh in his motor boat when the fog came in. He had sat about for half an hour and then gave up as he felt that he would not be able to find the big boat when and if he found the Ray. He asked where was I going to start and I explained our plan to start at Foulness Island and tow down to the Warps buoy over the last of the flood. If we did a bit we could shoot back up, or if we did not catch enough we could steam down with the first of the ebb to other grounds.

"That sounds like a good plan," he replied. "I will join you."

Now at that time, talk of a Foulness Airport was on everybody's lips and Colin had done a lot of work on an adjacent new man-made island. They had recently finished installing an observation tower and had placed numerous buoys taking wave height readings all over the Maplin Sands. One of these buoys was in the middle of the tow. The good news was that it had a very small light on it so we were able to use it as a marker when fishing there. We shot away on the 6.5 point and would tow down to the 13 red point on the Decca.

The Decca, or to give it its full name, the Racal Decca Navigator system worked on radio waves. It was developed very near the end of the World War II when the Navy needed to be more precise in positioning its ships and aircraft for the invasion of Normandy. It is said that the first people outside of the forces to know exactly when the invasion started were the two scientists who had created the Decca. They had made a set of their own after the military had taken over its development and it came to life on D-Day morning. There were three channels in this system: Red, Green and Purple. Lucky for us in the Estuary, the system give us easy cross reference lines - east west was green and north south was red - so we had nice squares to work with, unlike down channel where they had very long diamonds to work with. Each set distance had a number and that number was then divided into tenths. This would then give an exact position, which was then cross referenced with a chart that had all the squares on it. It may sound complicated, but it was a revolution. No more straining your eyes looking for marks ashore or a timed compass course and having to remember that the north Oaze buoy on the Towers and the South Shoebury buoy on the chimney was a fast[3] or wreck.

---

[3] A fast is an unknown sea bed obstruction that has been caught and pinned the boat to the sea bed hence "to come fast." (No giggles please!

The downside to us older guys now is we still think "in Decca" and not latitude and longitude. You remember the numbers, i.e: 17.20 red and 32.20 green is a wreck just behind the Red Sand Towers. After watching those dials for so many hours, the numbers stuck. My father was a whiz at this and knew every wreck and fast on the Oaze and Red Sands by heart, reciting his tow as though he was reading it. He would get so cross with himself when he made a mistake and caught one, which he would do now and again. However, the readings did fluctuate at night a bit and it was very unreliable in a thunderstorm.

We shot away without a hitch and I thought we should tow in very shallow water just clear of the ebb a dry[4]. We made a good speed as the tide in the shallow water was far less than in the deep. We had to clear the observation tower as this was only just clear of the line we were taking and we passed it by a couple of boat-lengths. Colin shot on my offer quarter (with the sand on my inner side) and remained there for the whole tow. With the tide slackening, we were soon down the tow and started to haul as we closed the Warps beacon. The beams cleared the water and I gave her a burst of power then knocked her out of gear. I went to the starboard side to haul in my cod end, and I put the turns of the lazy decky[5] around the drum and pulled the cod end up to the rail. I then clipped on the tackle to haul the cod end out of the water, and with the water so clear I could see a couple of sole sticking in the meshes in the wings of my net. Just then my crew sang out that he had some big sole sliding back down the gear and he was trying to trap them against the rail. Next thing, a sole was thrown into the fish pound behind the mast. I could see my bag coming up and there were many "stickers." This is what we call the smaller sole whose heads stick through the net, hence the word stickers. As the bag came aboard, it was crackling - a sure sign it was full. Crabs were crawling out the meshes and falling on the deck in their hundreds and making this unmistakable crackle sound.

On opening the bag, many thousands of them fell to the deck making a big pile. Both nets were the same. We often see this when the water is clear, and the big pile soon drops, as the crabs sort themselves out and start walking up or down the deck looking to escape. We had cottoned on to this and would make openings for them to walk over the side. But the good news was that it was a good haul of sole with some real big ones, and not all slips.

---

[4]The ebb a dry is the edge of a sandbank, in this case the Maplin Sands which just dries out at low tide.

[5]The lazy decky is a rope that is used to haul parts of the gear on to the boat instead of by hand.

A net of stickers.

Slips are small Dover sole and are worth the least money. It is the big ones that fetch the best price, sometimes three times the price of the small. Colin was turning to shoot up as we did a sharp turn to head back up into the strengthening ebb tide.

I was a little ahead of the *Ina K,* so I chose the line and he had to stick on my port side quarter or tow where we had just been. We towed against a good ebb tide and we were soon picked up, a heaped basket: very nice. There was no waste and no weed, just the crabs all very clean. Normally the ebb tide brings more rubbish from off the top of the Maplins as the water drains off. Colin called on the VHF and asked how had we done. I reported to him a heaped basket, he had just a basket.

This routine carried on all night, moving to the south just a little or a tenth on the Decca each haul. As daylight came the fishing collapsed from very good to nothing in just an hour. Colin did have another haul but he caught nothing. We went home very happy with what we had caught: 29 stone of sole. Yes, we were very happy indeed! The rest of the week continued in that vein. We worked shoulder to shoulder with Colin on virtually every haul. Ironically we beat him every day, not by much, but enough.

When Dad returned the next week, rested and fired up, he asked Colin: "Where should we make a start?"

"Don't ask me; ask your bloody son, he knows."

I took that as a compliment, and Dad, well I just saw him smile. As you will read in other stories, when the three of us worked together we caught fish and had some bloody good fun. The total age of the two of us on the *Anja* was 39 years, but we had graduated into a man's world.

Crew of the Greater London 2 (taken in the early 1970s).
Back row from left to right: Bob Chalk (alias Chalky); John Hipsey; Michael Rownan;
Bob Fossett; Paul Gilson.
Front row from left to right: Young Tom Thornton; Aubrey Martin; Peter Gilson (Dad,
wearing slippers as usual); Derrick Tyler; Tom Thornton senior (alias Old Tom).
In the foreground: Reginald Saunders (alias Diddles).

A Man's World

NOT LONG AFTER I started work, the telephone rang in the middle of the night, not that there was anything unusual in that. I heard Dad speaking. "Right, oh you call Tom, Derrick, Jim and Aubrey, and I will call Colin, Roy, John and Nigel and the train driver."

He started ringing out. "Roy, call for the boat, pick up Colin."

"You awake?" he shouted up the stairs.

"Yes," I replied.

"Come on, get dressed. You do a man's job, now you'll behave like one."

I had been waiting for this for so long, my clothes were on in seconds. Dad had made two more calls by the time I was at the bottom of the stairs. Dad was the coxswain of the Southend Lifeboat, and the youngest person to hold that title in the history of the modern service, I was told.

"You ring Bernard and Diddles. Just say 'call for the boat', you know the routine." I did. I had been watching this for years. I knew all these guys.

"Bernard, Paul Gilson here, call for the boat."

"Right oh."

Bernard was our train driver. We were the only lifeboat station with a train driver as part of the crew. After all we did have the longest pier in the world, with over a mile to go down. When I was older, I have ran and have even cycled down that bloody pier far too many times when someone had encouraged the train or buggy to leave without me.

"Cut the crap, they know who you are," Dad's voice from above shouted.

My next call was briefer: "Diddles, call for the boat." Diddles had been on the crew for ever. Reginald Saunders was his full name, but it was never used. He was the second engineer. He could tell a good rescue story, sometimes more than once, but he had been there and done that.

Dad came down the stairs, grabbed his car keys, put on his slippers (which he wore everywhere) and we were out the door.

"Blast!" Back in he went. "Forgot me fags," he said, jumping into the car and we were off down the road like a rocket.

There were no seat belts then, they were not even fitted. In no time we were on the sea front, bombing along. This is great fun I thought, seeing another car behind us with headlights blazing, coming at speed. Up on the pavement next to the pier were three cars already, someone behind us, people in states of undress and someone with his head stuck in a jumper.

"What is it Pete?" they were asking.

"Someone on a ship in the anchorage[1] is hurt; they need us to take him off." Not quite true as it turned out. The lights came on in the station and as the doors were being unlocked, two cars arrived from Leigh and another from Shoebury.

"That looks like the lot," Dad said.

With that, a great Mercedes bumped up the curb.

"You better wait a bit for Percy," he called to Bernard the train driver, as we ran to the first coach.

"Don't wait for me," Percy shouted. "I will ride in the cab at the back."

This was Percy Garon, a legend in his own lifetime, and a man whom I had known since I could walk. A genuine great man, who was awarded the Military Medal of the First World War. He told me a story of driving a car across no-man's land loaded with injured soldiers. The car had a hand throttle and it got shot away. He had no choice in the matter - he just aimed the car where he wanted to go and hoped it got there. His superiors were so impressed that they sent him out again to bring a convoy across no-man's land the next night. It got blown to bits. Percy and a few others survived. I only ever got that story the once; it was never mentioned again. He ran the fire service in Essex during the Second World War and then ran a large catering business in Southend. I am told he was chauffeur-driven from Southend to the fire service Chelmsford HQ in a blackout and air raid in just 16 minutes.

One Sunday morning when I was about five years old, Dad had taken me with him down the pier and there was a call. I was not allowed to go because I was far to young, so I threw a big strop.

---

[1] *The anchorage is an area put aside for ships to anchor awaiting orders or a berth to unload. To see a ship at anchor now is rare, but in the late 1960s you would often find 20 ships anchored off Southend and Shoebury.*

Percy Garon retired in his eighties. Here he is at his retirement party being presented by Dad with a ceremonial hammer identical to the one used to launch the lifeboat.

Percy told me I had to be brave as my father had a job to do and I would be going out with him soon. This did not stop me being a pain, but the offer of an ice cream did the trick. He took me ashore to one of his shops, and brought me a very large ice cream. Percy felt that it would make me feel better. He was right. I did not know then that he owned the shop and most of the high street.

Some years later when I had became a helmsman, I had an argument with one of the older hands. I threatened him with a smack on the nose. I had to be disciplined for my behaviour and was summonsed to see Percy, with no protection from my Dad now. I went to his big house on the seafront, and was let in by Percy's wife who then pointed to a large door. I entered a big room with a huge table in it with Percy sat at the head. I was directed to stand at the end. He proceeded to cut me down. He did it in such a way I could have walked under the door. He firmly put me in my place and not once did he raise his voice. But before I turned into a quivering jelly, he rebuilt me bit by bit, and restored my confidence. It was the worse telling off I had ever had, yet the best, from a truly a great man.

Today was the day I was moving from a boy's world to a man's one. The last ten minutes had been hectic, yet here we sat chatting as the train thundered down the pier at 11 mph but it was flat out. We arrived at the south station and the running began again.

"Take the keys and open the door," Dad said.

I was off like a shot. No sooner was the door open, the rest of the crew were behind me, some went left and some right. I was sent right to help Jim load up the boots, oil skins and life jackets. Jim operated the radar on the lifeboat. He ran the radar school that was based at the end of the pier and was very good. He worked during the later part of the Second World War with the radar pioneer Watson Watt, who was out of place as a seaman but made up for it with his expertise. On one lifeboat mission we were looking for a downed aircraft. Despite huge flocks of seagulls filling his screen he guided us to a contact from several miles away. This contact, he assured us, was metal. And it was - a metal chair frame, with one leg sticking out of the water by six inches. Jim was bloody good.

The great big winch was fired up and the slack taken up on the wire, her platform tilted. The safety chains were taken out through the keel and the engines burst into life. Everyone seemed to be finished with their job except Jim and I.

"That will do," someone said.

"There are only eight of us on board," another one noted.

So I followed the others up the steps and was sent below.

"Keep out of the way," Dad said to me. "Everyone onboard?"

No reply.

"Okay Bernard, when you're ready"

There was a brief pause as Bernard unscrewed the safety pin and then:

"Okay?"

"Okay," Dad replied.

There was a big clang as Bernard hit the release pin with his hammer quickly followed by another as the hook hit the deck. The lifeboat started to move, slowly at first but gathering speed quickly. There were squeals as some of the rollers in the groove of the slipway were reluctant to turn. Whoosh, water went every where. Dad put the power on and two men lowered the rudder as another two put up the mast. Radios burst into life

"Southend Coastguard, Southend Lifeboat launched on service."

"Roger, Southend Lifeboat."

"Proceed to…."

The message was interrupted. It was not for me. Tea was more important and that was to be my job for years.

"Paul?" called Dad.

"Yes."

"Put the kettle on."

We had all mod cons on the *Greater London 2*. We had an electric kettle! There still was a primus stove for boiling the water but we had moved on: we had a proper kettle, a tea pot and tinned milk. Over the years I did try to make a good cup. But to be honest it was pretty grim, thankfully no one complained. It was, after all, hot and sweet and if we were out for any length of time the rum as it was shared out. The tea became irrelevant, just a mixer. Later on we had powdered pre-made drinks: 'just add hot water'. I considered that my tea was very good in comparison.

We were tasked to a tanker that was anchored near the South Shoebury buoy. She was, I think, from Scandinavia, possibly Norwegian. It was a flat calm, a very nice night. Southend Pier was soon well behind us and the tea was made, a 'well done boy' and 'thanks youngster' came from the men as I passed round the tea.

I often wondered if Dad was doing what I do when I take people out that are lost for something to do. You try to make them feel useful, give them a job, make the tea. We were soon at the ship, her lights sparkled and reflected on the water giving an eerie glow. We were soon alongside her. The tanker looked huge from our deck with so many lights glaring away. Ropes were passed and we had two of our men quickly aboard. Dad had sent Aubrey as he was our top first-aider. After just a few minutes the other hand called down asking for the stretcher.

"What's the score?" Dad called out.

"Tell you shortly," he replied.

He disappeared, then came back on board a few minutes later. He was not going to shout. He went in to the wheelhouse with Dad and they spoke quietly for what seamed like an age. He scuttled back up the companion way. Dad called us all together.

"The man is dead, he has been cooked," he said. "Now for some of you it may be the first time you have seen a dead man. He did not hurt you before he died and he will not hurt you now. The boys are wrapping him up before they lower him down in the stretcher. If it upsets you keep on the starboard side."

That little speech was probably just for me but the others knew the score.

They remained silent, they had all been there and done that. The body was gently passed down and onto the lifeboat; it was wrapped in plastic sheets. We slipped the ropes and got underway for the pier. I felt sick and a terrible sadness. I wanted to cry, but thought I must put on a brave face. I couldn't let Dad down.

As we closed the pier, Jim had radioed ahead for an ambulance and the crew were waiting at the boathouse. Dad put her alongside the slipway and several of us carried the body up the slip to a buggy that was used to move heavy stuff around the pier. It was all very quiet, none of the usual banter. While we had been doing this, some of the crew were getting out the mooring lines that would help Dad put her back in the slipway. One rope to the east and another to the west, all rowed out from a large skiff.

We climbed back on board and let go the pier. We made a big sweep round and picked up the up tide line. Dad kicked her ahead and let her stern go up before checking the rope. We picked up the other rope and tried to line her up to the slipway. With just a few hand signals we were on the slip and a few bumps in the groove.

A heaving line was thrown out to us and the retrieving wires secured, the rudder was pulled up and with another hand wave, the great electric winch started to pull her up, a little jerky at first but smoother as she cleared the water.

The engines were stopped by another hand signal and the bow ropes released for recovery. About half way up the winch was stopped and the springs were placed over the two bits aft. The springs strained and groaned as the weight of the boat came on them. Already some of the crew were starting to climb down to get the water and soap ready to wash her down. The mast and aerials were lowered and secured; the main wire was pulled off and reattached to the fitting below, the rudder and at the end of the keel. A check was made, all clear was shouted and she started back up the slip.

It was still very quiet to what was the norm. There were crew now on both sides washing and cleaning her down. She must look her best for when the public comes to see her. The life jackets and boots that we had put on earlier went back in their racks and oilskins were hung up, she was back on the cradle and that was tilted back so she was level. The safety chains were in place and before you knew it, all was done.

If it was not for the water everywhere you would not have known she had been out, the service board was updated and it was time to go home. It was still very quiet for what was normally a rowdy bunch.

As the last man out turned off the power to the winch and the lights, Dad shut the door and locked it. We walked round the pier to the station and onto the train, no one running about this time. We boarded the train and the doors closed. Then someone broke the spell.

"What happened then, Aubrey?"

Aubrey took a deep breath.

"The guy's girlfriend was with him on the ship, they had been having a drink and they had a big argument. She went to bed and he went to the sauna to sober up. He turned the heat up and then collapsed against the door. She woke to find him not there and went to look for him; she raised the alarm, the rest you know."

Cooked, I thought, what a way to go!

"Bloody women," said a voice from the end of the coach. "They have a lot to answer for."

Grunts of agreement echoed around the coach. Very much a man's world, I thought, but that would be changing soon. Back to the cars and we were all off home. Daylight was already coming in the east.

Perhaps I would get another hour's sleep. I doubted it.

Paul (left) and Dave Witton on a shoot.

Best friend Darren.
He constantly bumped his head going into the wheelhouse on the Janeen.

Joker

OVER THE YEARS I have been known to be a bit cruel to some friends and relations, but the outcome was always funny - well, at least to me.

Just after we brought the *Anja*, Dad would often do a fishing party, taking a few friends or sometimes paying anglers. This particular day it had been arranged by a second cousin of mine, Dave Witton. Dave and his family lived next door to where my mother was brought up in Little Wakering. Dad knew Dave's dad well, he worked the Roach for oysters and did a bit of fishing and we would visit them on Sunday afternoons. Dave has a lot to answer for; he used to let me ride on the tank of his motorbike. Up and down his road we would go, with me begging for more. Kimberly Road must have been one of the last roads to be made up in Essex, it was so very bumpy but it was great for a five-year-old. He was also the person who introduced me to shooting. At the end of Kimberly Road, Wakering Creek starts and the fun of duck shooting started for me at the age of eleven. I had been keen to shoot for some time and Dad had bought me the smallest shotgun around. It was called a garden gun, the small cartridge was no bigger than a ink cartridge in a pen but to me it was huge. It had only one barrel and was a bolt action and I was taught how to use it. The first time I pulled the trigger it was at a turkey, well a picture of one on the box that our Christmas bird came in. It was in the back garden and it just managed to tear the cardboard.

The evening eventually came when Dave picked me up to go to flight (the term used for the evening or morning movement of birds) and we walked from his dad's house to the marshes at the end of the creek. He gave me another lecture about safety and what not to do. Something that has held good for many years, but we can still make mistakes and get carried away. We made our way to the bend in the creek and we lay behind the sea wall waiting for the ducks to fly over. I remember we could hear them flying about but they were not coming close enough to see, let alone shoot at. However in a flash, and I do not remember shooting it, a teal cleared the sea wall and I shot it even before Dave got his gun to his shoulder. The duck fell to the ground alongside us and bounced about a bit and died. The exclamation from Dave I can not describe but the TV character Victor Meldrew would have summed it up with: "I don't believe it". I will be honest - I was surprised as well. It must have only just cleared the top of the sea wall. Any further away and for me it would have been out of range. It would be many years before I would get the hang of it, but shooting with Dave was great fun. One Sunday after the morning flight, his mum cooked me the biggest and best fry up I had ever had. I commented that it was so good I could eat it again. As we cleaned our guns I was summed back to the table. She had cooked the whole meal again. I did not waste a mouthful - it was just as good as the first meal if not better. Dave's father Jack just lowered his Sunday paper and smiled.

"Dave often had two breakfasts when he was your age," he said.

Dave was also fishing mad, he belonged to a fishing club and it was his club we were taking out. Dave was and still is very excitable. He is the only person I know who gets excited about the football results being read out on the radio. He was at this time on a diet, his partner had been nagging him about being fat and there was a new diet going round, as there always is. He was following The Hard Boiled Egg and Celery Diet. According to Dave, it made you a bit windy but it did fill you up. We had been anchored for some time and the fishing was slow. It was cold outside and Dave had come into the wheelhouse to eat his food while still watching his rod. Now Dave was fishing the starboard side, so he was watching from that window, under which the switches and fuses for the lights for the whole boat were mounted. Dave produced a half dozen box of eggs, all hard-boiled. He selected one and used the switchboard case to crack it. After eating several eggs, he put the box back in his bag and went back out to do some more fishing, while munching on some celery. I could not resist it. I went to my food cupboard and removed two eggs, brown the same as Dave's.

Dave was busy catching a cod and I changed two hard boiled eggs for two fresh ones. Dad saw me at Dave's bag and asked what was I doing.

"Just watch," I replied.

Dave came back in and wiped his hands, boasting about the lovely fish he had just caught. He went to his bag and out came the eggs. Again, he cracked an egg on the frame again with some gusto and peeled it, and then took another stick of celery and munched away. As it was a large stick, he took another egg from the box and smashed it on the frame.

It exploded everywhere! Both he and Dad went potty. The wheelhouse erupted with noise: Dad was having a go at Dave; Dave was calling his partner Brenda a silly cow; and egg yoke was running down over the switch panel. I was nearly wetting myself. After what was like an age, with Dave begging forgiveness and much cleaning up, an inquest took place on how Brenda could have made such a stupid mistake.

All calmed down and we concentrated on catching fish, but Dave was still chewing a brick over the egg. I had to go and make some tea. I could hardly contain myself as another one lay in wait for him. Time was getting on and we packed up and headed for home. I was cleaning down the decks and helping the anglers gut their fish. I was beginning to think that Dave would not eat any more, just in case it happened again, but Dave loved his food - he would not let me down.

I went and stood at the back of the wheelhouse while they chatted about football and Dave went for his bag. I had a flash of guilt, a touch of remorse, but it only lasted a second as he picked the egg up. He stopped and started talking again. The suspense was killing me. Would he break it or not take a chance? No, Dave loved his food. Down came his hand with the egg, one crack and it went everywhere again, probably worse than last time. I cried! Poor Brenda, what he called her is not worth mentioning. For days Dad had fun ridiculing Dave and and even his mates were laughing.

About a week later, I could not hold it back any longer. I rang Dave, explained and tried to apologise. He was not best pleased. When he had gone home that day, they'd had a blazing row. Brenda had threatened to leave him and if they had been married, a divorce would have been on the cards.

Sorry Dave! And really sorry Brenda, but it was very funny I hope you can laugh about it now.

I did the same thing again in that very wheelhouse many years later, when I was the *Anja's* skipper. We had a young lad with us called Darren Stag. He could not wait for the holidays to come out with us. He was boat bonkers. It did not matter what shape or type it was, he was interested and he loved coming out with us. Now, Darren was about 14 years old and he had a sweet tooth like most youngsters. He had been taking an extra chocolate biscuit when we were hauling and an odd sweet when I took some on board. It did not matter to me but it left him wide open to be trapped - and trap him we did. Now Dad was a soft touch for silly pens and plastic screwdrivers and mini spanners. It was nothing strange to find a fried-egg pen or dog-poo pen kicking about, but today I knew the one I needed: a chocolate Flake pen. We were having short hauls and were in and out the wheelhouse all the time. I told my crew what I was doing.

He smiled. "Surely he won't fall for it?"

"You watch," I replied.

I had a small paper bag and put the Flake inside with about an inch showing and tucked it in the corner or the wheelhouse where I normally left the biscuits. I unscrewed the wheelhouse light so the only light was from the instruments - enough to just make out what was in there, but not enough to read. The trap was set and we hauled. Because Darren was so young I would not let him be on deck in the dark when we were hauling so he was left in the wheelhouse. He had several minutes to be caught and he was, when the bags came on deck he could come back outside. When he came out he was holding his jaw

"What's the matter?" I asked.

"A bit of toothache" he replied, as he rubbed his jaw.

When we had shot again I checked out the bag, the Flake was still there but not as I had left it. I took it out the bag and there were two teeth marks about two inches down the stick. My crew came in and asked: "Well?" I showed him the pen/Flake. He smiled with the words: "Got him".

We never lost another biscuit or sweet again. I made a friend, and he was my best friend for many years, only to be cut short by Darren's untimely death at 41.

I told this story at his funeral; but it is very hard to laugh at a funeral.

Bruno v Tyson

IT WAS THE end of February 1989 and a full moon; bad weather was forecast but at the moment it was fabulous. We had decided to go to sea and get the high water haul in on the Herring Bank, which is located off Herne Bay. The bank is a few miles east of Whitstable and about a mile off shore. We had an order for 200 stone of herring at a fair price, and since it was so close to home and virtually at the end of the season, we decided would go for it. Depending on weather conditions, the herring spawn there from about the end of February through to middle or even the end of March.

Tonight was not an ordinary night for Ron, the skipper of the other boat. It was a very big night: Frank Bruno was fighting Mike Tyson. Ron loved boxing and was no slouch himself, but he started too late in life to realise his full potential. A strong left hand and large fist were his tools and a bent nose was his trophy. It was live on telly and Ron had taken one on the boat especially for the occasion. I left Southend at about 11pm to drive down to Whitstable, picked up my crew for the night and headed off toward the Dartford Tunnel hoping to be home before the next morning's rush hour. The roads were empty and with the full moon it was one of those rare events, a pleasurable drive. Once through the tunnel and along the motorway the Kent countryside was bathed in moonlight and was quite stunning. Arriving at the quay side in Whitstable the other boats were already getting under way. We had company: "needy and greedy" or "The Greedies" to their friends; otherwise known as Steve and Charlie. They obviously had an order too. The tide had just come in and they floated before us, so we would have someone out there looking for the fish before we got out there, not a bad thing, may save us a bit of time.

Ron was already aboard, his boat's engine running and telly on. We said our greetings and I started the *Janeen* up and I followed Ron out. The scene of us leaving the harbour was something quite moving. It has been going on for centuries yet seeing fishing boats going to sea has something about it I cannot describe. Perhaps it was just the light that evening that set it off, and I saw clearing the harbour how the moon sparkled on the water.

I commented to Ron how beautiful it was and how everything was sparkling. He replied that all he wanted to sparkle was Bruno's fists. His mind was not on the job, as we steamed off toward the Street buoy where the "Greedies" were already shooting away. Ron went towards them and I steamed further down river, looking for the spawning fish. The others were working quickly. Ron asked them what they could see because he could see nothing on his fish finder. Nor could they was the answer. Did we know that a force 10 was forecast? Err, no. They had shot and were going to tow a line where the fish had shown the previous day. A bit risky, but if that weather was indeed due, it was a game plan. We steamed around a bit but saw very little. Ron was giving us all a running commentary of the start of the fight but we had not seen a mark worth talking about. We went a bit further to the north and toward the mouth of the River Swale. Ron suggested we shoot down as well and go through the motions as the fish should come to us. As we were shooting away a little wind came up from the east, but not much, just an air - it was still a very picturesque evening. Towing to the east, we were making good speed. Then a gentle swell started to come from the east but no wind, yet. A few marks started to show on the sounder like Quality Street wrapped sweets, gold on a blue background. Not much at all, so the kettle was on and tea was imminent.

The commentary was coming thick and fast over the radio and occasionally some talk of fish. Brum, my crew that night, went outside to answer the call of nature. He came back in and said: "Corr blimey Paul, it's blowing a gale out there. I have only just filled the kettle and there was not any sign of it then."

Within five minutes, the *Janeen* was putting her head under and water was running down the deck. I could clearly see the waves breaking over Ron's boat, some going over the top of her wheelhouse. Ron wasn't bothered, as Bruno was doing well - he had hit Tyson very hard, but just not hard enough, I was told. "I am starting to see some good marks, Ron."

"He's not doing too bad, he's in with a chance."

"Nice show here now, Ron."

"Oh, he's taking some punishment but he's holding up okay."

"Have you seen any thing there?"

"No, just aeration."

When it gets rough air bubbles form under the boat, it is called aeration and it gives a false picture on the fish finder.

"It's getting quite good now."

"He's down."

"This is getting good."

"He up, I think he's cut."

"If we can hold this for ten minutes we should have enough. Ron, if we turn round we can go through those marks again and then haul with the sea, it's pretty bad out there."

"You want to see this, he has some guts but he's not good enough to beat him. I cannot see a thing its too rough for my set and the water is going over the boat."

"Round me then?"

"Okay."

Holding what was left of my tea we turned round off to the north. Was it only ten minutes ago that we said it was calm? After rolling around, we settled to tow with the sea and what was left of the tide. Waves were going past us and were quite big considering the depth of water.

"I have some marks coming."

"Just aeration here," Ron said.

"I think we should haul Ron. I am seeing a very good mark here."

"I don't think he's going to make it."

"I have just been outside it's grim out there, and it's too rough to haul. We'd better pull up towards home and it might improve. It is not getting any better here, that's for sure. If anything, it is getting worse," I replied.

With the wind and waves pushing us along we were soon passing where we had shot. The other boats had hauled and were on their way back in. We were into fish again.

"Ron, I am seeing some very good marks again, but I am getting concerned!"

"It's much too rough out there, but let's go a bit further," said Ron. "If we haul now we could do a lot of damage. Oh, that was a big one and again I don't know how he standing up after that."

"If we don't do it soon we will loose the gear. I have seen a lot of fish, we will just lose the gear or the cod end at least. "

"Come on, let's do it, we will run out of water soon," said Ron, who had his eyes fixed on the fight. "He is taking some pounding; it is only his guts keeping him in there. We are ready, we will come close and haul up to the ends then come together and pass the ends over and I will get out of the way."

That sounded so easy, but we had a full gale now, water was breaking over the sterns of both boats and boxes were moving about the deck. This was not going to be a routine hauling session; if we hit each other in these conditions, despite having many fenders on our sides, we would and could do some serious damage. Brum opened the door of the wheelhouse, saying: "This could be fun," and laughed in a way that only he could.

At this time we had a net hauler on the stern, a large grooved wheel into which you drop the end of the net and then just pull down. The wheel then turns and grips the net. Hopefully this would work tonight, because pulling it aboard by hand was out of the question. As we came together, water was breaking and blowing past us, we were along side for just a few minutes. The ends were soon over and made fast. Ron's crew were on deck with mine and the stern and bow ropes released. He was gone in no time, I should have realised then why he was away so quickly - we weren't moving.

We started to pull down on the hauler but the net was not coming aboard, there was too much weight, the wind and the waves and our catch was working against us. I would have to try and help by coming astern but I could not afford to let her come round side to the weather. Ron in the meantime was off home, the boxing was still going on. We were struggling; the waves were higher than the gantry as we dropped into the seas. Waves were hitting the stern and breaking all over the boat, the boys were working hard to control the gear.

"There is more fish than we need," was the cry from aft.

"We will only just get the retrieving rope," Tim, my other crewman, shouted. "Try and give her a kick round so we can get the bag alongside."

I tried, there was so much fish the net had a mind of its own. Standing up straight was a problem let alone getting fish aboard. The crew managed to get the sleeve on to her starboard side, it was only a short sleeve but it was full, probably between eight to ten tons. The boat was rolling heavily and it was hard work keeping your feet steady.

"Another kick, Paul, we can hold it," said Tim.

Try as I might, she would not come round and it looked as though we would lose it. She then stuck her stern into a big wave, gripped the water and she started to slide to port bring the gear along the starboard side.

We were very fortunate that we had good crew, but they still struggled.

"Another kick. We cannot hold them."

"Got it!" The bag was hooked on the tackle, it lifted and there was a squeal. I was too slow. The sleeve had found the propeller. The great sausage of fish had rolled under the boat as we had lifted, now we were up against it.

"Don't worry," I said. "Get the bag up and we will see what we can do." Now the bag was full, it had been stretched with the extra weight.

"No choice, it's got to come aboard."

We were losing fish from the hole we must have made with the prop but it was not easing the weight enough to help. As the bag left the water it was indeed a big one, very big. "Keep clear every one, just in case." The bag was so big it was pulling the boat over to meet it. Tim looked at me with eyes that said: "Well?"

"Keep going," Brum said.

"It's huge, it will pull us over."

With that she rolled and it flopped aboard. It was huge.

"Oh ye of little faith," I said smiling. When the bag opened, the fish poured along the deck. We were listing heavily to starboard but okay. I quickly called Ron on the VHF to put him in the picture.

"I am alongside," he said. "Bruno lost."

"I have the net round the prop and several tons of fish alongside so don't go home yet."

"See what you can do."

Fish were still spilling out, we did not need any more. The sleeve had been made fast aft and we had the bag aboard. "We will have to tear it off, there cannot be that much round there."

Tim had put a strop around the sleeve above the bag and put the tackle on it. When he had it tight, he looked at me. "Okay I will give her a kick and see what happens."

I gently put her astern, she made a grunt and the sleeve was free. Fish was floating all round her, but we still had fish in the sleeve. We gathered the torn end up, but it was just too rough. We thought we had what we needed on deck, so we let the rest go. "It's off, but I think we have some still around it. I think we have enough fish for what we want," I said.

Ron went on and on about the fight. "Yes Ron," was all I could muster.

The boys were getting stuck in to the fish before I got underway.

"Just get enough boxed up to balance her up," I said. "Then get off the deck and I will jog in, we can box up in the harbour."

We were soon in the shelter of the harbour, having screwed and rolled our way in, while the boxed herring slid about the deck like old bumper cars. We landed nearly 300 stone from that one bag. We have not done it since. The demand for herring is now so poor that it is not worth catching and even if we had a market the amount of quota we have would not support a targeted fishery. This is a shame, as it is good tasty food and what I have been observing recently there is no shortage of fish. I had to get a diver to clear the propeller the next day; the hole was big enough to get a bus through but we put a patch in and it was good as new.

It is like a dream now; we were only at sea about three hours in total and so much happened. I have made much of Ron watching the boxing, which is all true, but the professional team we had with us made it happen. We would now find it difficult to have crew of the quality we had that day, with restricted fishing opportunities we are not getting the quality young people that the industry needs to support itself.

I got home around seven, as the kids were getting ready for school.

"Bit rough out there Dad?" Jo asked.

"Not too bad," I replied.

"You're covered in scales! They look like sequins," Julia exclaimed.

"Egg and bacon?" Heather asked.

Now that was back to reality and my bed was calling.

This is how I remember this night's fishing but talking to Tim and Jason, a crew from the other boat recently, they remember it differently. They think we had a running commentary from another boat. Some names have been changed in the telling of this story.

Heather

HEATHER, MY WIFE, and I have been together since we were 15, and she was still at school when I started work. When we got together she knew I was fishing mad and about my involvement with the RNLI. I proposed to her when we were 18 and we married at 19. Why, you may ask, does this fit with my stories of fishing? Well this story is about going fishing with Heather.

Heather and I met at a lifeboat dinner dance at the Halfway House function rooms on the seafront at Thorpe Bay, it was 7th February 1969. The weather that night started well but became a gale with blizzard conditions. The lifeboat was called about 10pm, when nearly all the crew were there dressed in lounge suits and the ladies in their best frocks - after all, it was a dance. The lifeboat on duty was an old reserve boat serving out her last years before being sold off, but it was a real lifeboat. She was probably pre-war or just after, which meant there was no shelter - only a dodger to protect the crew- and no comforts like the *Greater London*.

The crew all charged off leaving, all the wives, girlfriends and their guests behind. This actually was to my advantage being the boy amongst my peers, the micky-taking and good humoured banter that the youngest of a gang gets was taken away. There were two young girls there, Jill and Heather. I had brought my best friend at the time Steve T, all of us 15. Steve went after Jill, and I, Heather. We could have a dance without interference or being under someone's critical eye. I cannot dance, but by the end of the evening we had several shuffles around the dance floor and I had a date sorted. While we were having so much fun, Dad and his crew were battling the elements, a gale, blizzard conditions and sub-zero temperatures. He was to say many times it was the coldest he had ever been in his life, but at that time it was just wasted talk to me. Years later, I was to find out for myself what it was to be at sea in an open boat doing 30 knots in sub-zero conditions. I was that cold, it was difficult to bend my hands, which felt like they had been replaced by bananas - but that is another story.

Heather and I started out our courtship by doing the normal stuff - pictures once a week, a Chinese meal after the film and lots of walking. I had left school that April and had started work, so compared to my mates I was rich. Heather and I parted for a little while, but by mid-summer we were back together, and it was fish that made it happen. Dad's boat was in Leigh having a paint up when Heather came sailing alongside. She had been fishing in the creek and had caught several flounders. She was just being polite and came to say hello and show off her catch. She liked boats, she could sail and liked fishing, she would even dig her own bait. The romance was back on so it was no surprise that we went fishing together, mullet fishing to be precise, before she finished her summer holidays. And it would come as no surprise that she was able to start by hand a twin-cylinder Lister diesel engine.

At first there were three of us but for most of the week, it was Heather and I. We would use a ring net, a very old way of fishing but ideal for catching mullet. The net was about 100 yards long and we would lay it out in a dinghy and row it around a shoal of fish. Heather would take one end and a rope sweep and I would row out the sweep then the net to surround a shoal. I would then row for the bank and pull the net back to the shore closing the distance to where Heather was doing the same, a primitive purse seine[1]. It worked well, we worked the Ray (a deep channel that runs along the coast off Southend and runs up to Benfleet when the tide is in).

Mullet look a bit like bass and love the shallow warm water that we have so much of locally. They lay up in the Ray, and when the tide is out, they are forced into shoals while they wait for the returning tide. We would use one of the family's motor boats to tow the skiff up and down the Ray looking for the tell-tale sign of a tail disturbing the water as they swim in the shallows, a kick, a swirl or a jump. At the end of August and beginning of September their numbers would swell as they started to make bigger shoals, preparing to leave our shores bound for warmer climes of West Africa. We had caught several boxes on the ebb but this was nothing out of the ordinary, so we headed down the Ray towards Southend Pier for the flood tide.

---

[1] A seine is a large fishing net that hangs vertically in the water by means of floats at the top and weights at the bottom.

The problem is that the bank you pull into is over half a mile away. The tide goes over the mud flats and you have to pull to a row of mussel banks near the shore, whereas when you work the Ray you have a bank to pull to so much easier. Sure enough, we saw a large number of fish getting together to head for the shallows and we surrounded them. That was the easy bit. We now had to pull the net in and still surround the shoal of fish that was swimming along in front of the net, unaware that they were slowly being overhauled by the net and two teenagers. The tide was flowing and we had to go faster than the tide. We had a lot of fish in front of the net but we had not caught them yet, and we had a long way to go. Then we had our first cross words.

"Come on Hev, pull harder," I shouted.

"Don't you shout at me," was the quick reply.

We were slowly closing the net and the shore, where the motor boat was left on an anchor, now some distance off-shore and that would be a good row by the time we get hauled. The fish were now getting to realise that they were surrounded and many were jumping over the top of the net to escape. We were only in a few inches of water but they were getting away in good numbers.

"Come on, pull harder, close the gap not far now," I yelled.

"If you shout at me again, you will pull this in on your own," was the sharp retort. There was no doubt she was pulling her heart out. We made the mussel bank and shut the net. They could not escape now, we had them; oh there was a lot - well, a lot for two kids anyway.

There was a story that Lol and Dad had a shoot and could not get to the shore because there were too many and had to wade out and cut the net in half to manage to get a landing. They still had over 150 stone from half a net. We did nothing like this but they were four adults and had a bigger net than we were using.

I had been with Lol several times doing this job and hard work it was, but it was fun. We were laying the net back in the dinghy one day and the tide was round our feet but only a few inches deep. A fish was disturbed along the shore and it came toward us at speed. Lol trapped it with his foot just like a football, most impressive.

However, Heather and I had a good catch and only just managed to get all our fish and gear back in the dinghy and row out to the motor boat.

Our earnings were £60 each for the week. Not bad for two teenagers who would have done it for fun. I have never shouted at Heather again.

*Paul with full beard, posing for this picture and obviously not on service,
as he has his best shoes on.*

Two Men on the Boom

ONE EVENING ABOUT 11pm, I had just gone to bed when the beeper sounded. I was out and dressed quickly and very soon driving along the seafront. It was quite windy, about a 6 SW, as I remember. We arrived at the pier to be told: "*21* to the Boom[1], boat in difficulties." This 21 ft rigid inflatable lifeboat is commonly called a RIB, but we called it the "*Atlantic 21*" or just the "*21.*" It was designed by Atlantic College in Wales and revolutionised the lifeboat service.

There was nothing spectacular about the launch or the ride down river to the casualty, the tide was ebbing and it was not that rough. We quickly found the yacht, it had sunk and was wedged alongside the Boom. One of the occupants had climbed up the mast and was clinging on for dear life. He was very reluctant to come down as the boat was awash but I pushed the bow of the *21* on to the deck and put her nose on the mast, he then was convinced to climb down.

"Where is your crew?" we asked. "We were told there were two of you."

"Up there," he said pointing.

Our eyes went up and sure enough, sitting on top of one of the big piles that make up the Boom was a man, crouched like a gargoyle on some old cathedral. He had climbed up there when the boat had first hit the Boom. But now the tide was dropping and the boat had sunk, he was left literally high and dry. We were the wrong side of the Boom to get at him.

---

[1] *The Boom was built as part of the defence of the Thames from invasion in the Second World War. It runs from the Shoeburyness shore to the deep water where a net is strung from one side to the other. It is formed of a line of concrete plies driven into the sea bed, not far enough apart to allow a boat through. Over the year, it has saved many a windsurfer and yachtsman - as people start to get swept out to sea, it acts like a scoop to collect those drifting by.*

"Don't move! I will come round the other side," I shouted, with no idea if he heard me or not, but he didn't move. We had to go around the outer end of the Boom as it would have taken too long to go through the gap in shore.

When we approached him all I could think of was an old cormorant drying his wings sat on that pile.

"How are we going to get him down -he is scared stiff?" one of my crew said, concerned.

"Jump into the water?" the other one added.

We closed in on the Boom and instructed him to jump into the water and we would pick him up. A very quick "F. Off" reply was heard. We tried to talk him down, but to no avail,

"Okay," I said, "I will slide the 21 onto the hull."

"What?" was the gruff reply

"If Henry Blogg could do it, so can we," I told him, referring to Coxswain Henry Blogg from Cromer, the highest decorated lifeboat man in the RNLI, who had put a conventional lifeboat onto the deck of a casualty to rescue the survivors.

I put my plan into action, pushing the 21 onto the cabin top to raise the boat out of the water as far as I could so he could jump or climb down. The bow of the 21 was high out of the water possibly as much as a metre. I only hopped that we would not foul the props. After some coercing he climbed down and then jumped the last bit down on to the sponson, which is the large rubber tube that makes the side of the lifeboat and then into the boat. He was cold but okay.

Without much fuss we took them back to the lifeboat house where they had some tea and thanked us profusely for saving them. They had many bits of gear they needed to collect from their wrecked yacht and arranged to meet the coastguard later to walk out to her. We checked to see if I had damaged the boat and then made her ready for sea. We signed off and went home - just another job with a twist.

Some months later, I was reading my Sunday newspaper when a headline caught my eye: "Rescued Sailor Sues Owner." I read on and realised that this was my rescue. The crewman that we had rescued from the top of the boom was suing his mate for damages and the loss of his gear.

They seemed such a nice couple!

Child Drowning off Bell Wharf

THIS IS ONLY a short story. We were having our annual paint-up at Bell Wharf in Leigh. It was the middle of the summer and the place was heaving with people. Fortunately, given what was to happen this day, my boat was laying on the face and not the east side where I would have preferred her to be. It was very hot and the tide was coming in, the creek was packed with people swimming and paddling in the warm water. We had just had a tea break and were picking up our brushes, when I saw a child aged about five or six floating in the creek. He was face down and floating like a dead man, not moving at all. I could not quite gather what was happening - was he just doing a dead man's float, or was he drowning? One of my cousins, Glyn, was painting his boat in Bell Bay, and like me was in the lifeboat service. We realised that something was very wrong, but it was like slow motion.

"Where is his mum?" I called out. People were all around him but nobody was with him or appeared to care about him.

"Christ, he is drowning!" I shouted at Glyn. I dived off my boat into the creek, and as I swam under the water I could hear the child burbling. I came up underneath him, lifting him straight out of the water. My hand hitting him in the middle of the chest as I surfaced made him cough and gasp for breath. I dragged him toward Bell Bay where Glyn was wading out to meet me. Glyn carried him ashore and laid him down at the top of the beach next to the foreshore hut where the officer had already called an ambulance. The child coughed and spluttered, and then was sick. But still there was still no sign of a parent. An ambulance was soon there. It must have been passing as I had only just got to the top of the beach.

The paramedic said he would be okay, but they would stop with him for a bit. "Where are the parents?" he asked.

"No idea," we replied.

Cries came from along the beach. "My baby, my baby!"

I think now in hindsight that someone saw the look in our eyes as someone grabbed Glyn and I.

"Well done you two, let me buy you a drink!"

Quite literally we were ushered to the Smack pub and had what we would describe as a sharpener. Wet and trembling we tried to get our head round those few minutes.

I have often wondered what the mother was doing. That mother never said thank you and her son should be in his thirties now. I wonder if he remembers or even knew of what happened on that sunny day at Bell Wharf?

Having seen the same scenario several times in recent years, I put the following poem together, based on a true event that happened a couple of years back. I have called it Daniel, as that was what a mother was screaming out as she brushed the sand from her oiled body on the beach at Bell Wharf.

DANIEL

Daniel had come from afar
In his mum's new red car
They had come down to the beach
Swimming she was to teach

But she wanted to top up the tan
In an effort to please her new man
So Daniel was left on his own
Despite having a good old moan

So along the beach he did stray
Getting bored by the middle of the day
He saw the sea far away
And thought that's where he should play

Out on the mud he did walk
Not giving danger a second thought
Mum was happily laid on her back
Not giving a thought when he would be back

With tide fast coming in and Daniel so far out
No one would hear if he did shout
Mum was woken from her slumber
When someone rang her number

The tide had got to her feet
While she had been asleep
Of Daniel there was no sign
His body will show up in time.

Crew of the inshore rescue boat in the 1980s.
There were two of these boats - one at the north end of the pier to use when the tide was in
and another at the south end to use when the tide was out.
Paul is in the middle of the back row.

Lifeboat Near Misses

I AM ALWAYS CONCERNED when someone says: "I am never scared, nothing frightens me!" I would only reply: "Hum?" After a few lifeboat calls, I was asked if I was scared. "I could have been happier!" I would reply. Being scared and being brave are very close and yet miles apart.

In the early hours of the morning of the 21st October 1989, my beeper was activated. I woke to hear the wind banging on my windows and was quickly up and dashing to the pier. When I got there I was very surprised to see that the buggy had already gone with a full crew. The buggy was our personal means of transport down the pier. It was a converted golf buggy with a VHF radio, blue flashing lights and two-tone horns, with the capability to carry four people or two plus a stretcher.

Other members of the crew were still turning up. This did not make any sense to me, especially when the weather was this bad. I had been told I was the senior helm, so we made our way round to the inshore lifeboat house and opened up to listen to the radio and see what was going on. Now at this time we had three lifeboats at Southend: two at the end of the pier and one on the seawall at the north end of the pier. At the pier head we had an *Atlantic 21* (a rigid inflatable with twin outboards) and a D-class (all rubber construction with one 40hp outboard). On the shore we had a D-class, mainly for jobs along the foreshore and quick jobs close to home, a rapid response craft with shallow draft capabilities.

We learnt that one of the sand barges inbound for London had run aground near the South Shoebury buoy on the edge of the Maplins Sands and she was in danger of being swamped. It was indeed very windy, a good gale if not more. Soon after we saw the lights of the *Atlantic 21* Lifeboat leave the pier and then quickly lost sight of her as she disappeared in the troughs of what were very big seas. As much as I was not happy about what was going on, I could do little about it.

I suggested to those of us left behind that we should go home as there was little we could do. I told the Honorary Secretary (the Hon. Sec. to us) that there was little I could do here and my bed was a better place than being blown away standing on the seawall. As I left, the others on the wall stayed listening to what was happening out there. Waves were breaking and spray was floating about in the air. Not going to be too clever down there where they are going, I thought as I left the observer corps. When I got home the wind had indeed freshened, even in the short time I had been away. I was not too disappointed to be going back to bed. Heather stirred as I returned and asked: "False alarm?"

"No, I was pushed out," I replied grumpily.

"Never mind, you're welcome here," she said, as I slipped back into bed.

I was soon asleep. I have no idea for how long before I was woken again by the telephone ringing. I hit my head going down the stairs trying to get there as fast as possible so as not to wake my wife and children. I picked up the phone: "Hello?"

"You awake?"

"Yes!"

"We have a problem! Are you sure you are awake?"

"What is the problem?"

"The *Atlantic* has broken down and is drifting across the Maplins. They have the anchor down but it will not hold, they are drifting and she has nearly broached a couple of times."

While the Hon, Sec. was talking, I was looking out of my window watching the waves rush by and the local yacht club cruisers dancing on their moorings. What I was actually doing was working out the angle of the wind and sea. "The Sheerness boat cannot get to here and the helicopter is unavailable at this time," he told me.

My reply just came out matter of fact: "We can get it in the IRB, run down with the sea, tow her into the shore until she grounds and then pick her up in the morning. No risk, no heroics."

There was a stunned silence from the other end of the phone before he replied.

"Do you think? Who will you have with you, nearly the whole crew is here? How are you going to get the boat away, there is so much sea on the beach?"

"We can launch from the Prince Wales Beach, probably a bit of leeway there and I will see who is there when I get there, probably Clifton Warry and John Foster."

"Okay."

"Now what?" came a voice from the bedroom. Heather was awake.

"They are in trouble on the Maplins, broken down. I am going to go and get them in the rubber duck. Just going to tow them into the shallows and then they can walk home."

"Hum, you be careful."

"Of course I will."

I dressed for the second time that night, taking more care in what I was to wear, as I made my way up the steep steps in my back garden. The trees were dancing like characters in a Disney film. It was extremely windy. I did not rush this time on my way to the pier I kept looking out to sea and watching the waves crashing up the seawall and the spray falling on to the road. When I got to the boathouse there were people everywhere, and news from the lifeboat was not good. She had nearly capsized and her batteries were failing. John and Clifton had been told of what I had in mind but were not convinced. I would have to explain what I felt we could do and how we could do it. The three of us got into a car and we went around the wall to the beach were I felt we could launch from.

"That is going to be hairy," one of them said.

"Yes, but we can have people in their dry suits in the water on the beach. We cannot do that on the seawall, as it is steep and covered in weed, making it very slippery, the beach on the other hand is shallow and will give us a better grip."

We drove along the wall down towards Shoebury. I explained that as we went further to the east we would get the sea behind us. The only bad bit as I could see it was launching and getting enough sea room to get round the Boom.

"Okay I am in," said Clifton.

"Yep," said John.

"Sorry Paul, I just needed to see that you had thought this out and we were not just going gung-ho into the night," said Clifton. He was right. I would not be just going out on my own here, there would be other families at risk if I were to get it wrong. Clifton came from a yachting background, he knew what I could do. But he also knew that fishermen can be a bit reckless sometimes. We got back to the boathouse and every one started to get dressed in dry suits and life jackets. It was, as they say, "buzzing". We had explained to the Hon. Sec. our plans. It was after all on his head that the chopper would fall if we got it wrong. We had as many of the crew dressed in suits and jackets as we could but there were not enough suits to go round so some only had only life jackets to wear.

The communications with the *Atlantic* were poor but they had been told we were coming and to have a light ready. When we passed the end of the Boom, we would put up a flare so they would know we were there. There were not any lights in a D-boat so we would have to make our own. As we hurried along the seawall to the beach, pushing and dragging the trailer with the boat in it, the seas crashed on the wall and spume filled the air. The boat was so small compared to the waves that were hitting the wall.

"Don't worry, it will be different on the beach. They will be breaking but not as bad as these," I reassured the others.

It was by now a full storm, force 10, and the restriction on a D-boat was force 6 maximum. We put her on to the beach and I ran through what I intended to do. I would get in first and get her out of the trailer, spin her round and pick up the other crew. Everyone was to keep clear of the back of the boat as the propeller could remove a leg or foot just like that.

"Okay let's do it, " I said jumping in. The engine started first pull, the first wave lifted the boat high and the crew that were stationed around her side held her back in place. The next wave half filled the boat with water as I pulled her back out of the trailer. She was coming round a treat when another wave hit her on the side and up she went. Luck and judgment got her back. Another of the crew was in the right place and deflected her back to an upright position. John and Clifton jumped in and we were off straight into a wave, again we were swamped. Fortunately this helped us get clear of the beach as we were at water level, making it harder to get turned over.

"Thames Coastguard, Southend IRB launched on service," I reported.

The water drained quickly from the boat and we were soon well clear of the shore. The waves were big and I needed sea room, so I had to steam further out to get a good line to round the Boom. There was not much conversation at this time. We were playing with fire but so far, so good. I was driving the boat around the waves, never letting her come side to it or meeting a breaking sea head on. When I felt we had gone far enough to the south I let her come round and slowed up. "Everyone all right?" I asked.

I think Clifton said something deadpan like: "Well that was interesting." John had been on the VHF talking to the Coastguard. We would be called every five minutes just in case. It made me smile as it probably just made them feel better - if we went in it would have been over quite quickly, despite us being well dressed. But it was not going to happen.

"The *Atlantic* will put a flare up when we pass the Boom," John said. "The Mobile Coastguard unit can just hear them."

We could actually enjoy this bit running before the waves, this was good fun. Clifton was watching the waves behind me making sure a big one did not creep up on us. I am not sure who noticed it, but when we were in a trough we lost sight of the land. This was not something that we had much experience of in a D-boat. Even using a compass in one was considered very hard work; all navigation was done by eye. Running before such big waves was like surfing - you must not let the wave behind catch you or get too far ahead so you plough in to the back of the wave in front. Both could end in a capsize. We were all aware of that chance. I started to sing: "Oh we're riding along on the crest of a wave and the *Atlantic* is not here."

John laughed. "Shut up Gilson, do what you are good at - and it's not singing." We all laughed, gallows humour I suppose.

We passed the end of the Boom and called in on the VHF. It was too windy for me to hear what was being said but John passed on that the *Atlantic* would put up a flare. As if by magic we watched the rocket climb skywards then explode and the parachute deploy. As much as we tried we could not see the boat and it was still a long way to go. The coastguard relayed that the *Atlantic* was still dragging its anchor and they had all but broached a few minutes ago. The good thing now was that the water was getting shallower and the waves were past their best. We were making very good speed in what was near total darkness and after a few minutes we asked them if they could show a light for us to home in on. A pinprick of light appeared in the distance and we flashed a light back. John passed on that we had the *Atlantic* visual and in no time we were alongside. My first impression was that they had all been out on a huge bender in their oil skins and had woken up the next morning in the boat. That was how terrible they looked.

Some very good banter was exchanged between us, all of it unprintable! We took a line from them and they retrieved their anchor when we started to tow them ahead. We were making good headway and it was getting calmer. This was not because the wind had dropped but the water was now very shallow and waves could not develop. Instead of going straight ashore we towed them in towards the shore end of the Boom, until we started to touch bottom with the propeller. They had tilted their engines so we were still well afloat. I asked if the boys felt happy about walking her ashore and I would keep the D-boat afloat as the tide was dropping fast, they could then walk back to me. They thought it the best idea so there was no argument and five men pulling the boat soon disappeared toward the shore. This left me cruising up and down just keeping the boat afloat. There was a hint of light starting to show in the sky and many gulls were sheltering in the shallow water. With that I was over flown by a flight of widgeon just out of reach. They never fly that close when I am out shooting, I thought.

I could see John and Clifton wading back out to me and they were soon back in the boat. They had pulled the boat in until she had grounded and left the crew with her to walk ashore as they did not know what our ride back to station would be like. I had said we would just run ashore but with daylight coming I thought we could head back to the inshore shed. Keeping in the shallow water the waves would be very small and we would only just be afloat. We radioed our intentions to the Coastguard only to be told that the tide had already left the beach and the mud was showing. Another option was go to the end of the pier, but that was ruled out as stupid.

"Okay men," I said, "Although I said I was not going to do anything stupid, we have done what we set out to do and now we will go to East Beach and just get in as far as we can and walk home."

John passed this on and gave me the thumbs up. It was a strange experience in this growing light, passing through clouds of gulls and virtually flying along on a carpet of air as it was still very windy. With hindsight the boat was probably nearly airborne, but we weren't worried. It is only thinking about it now I realise how we were travelling more like a hovercraft than a boat. We rounded the Boom after quite a good steam; the speed we had gone down river had given us a false impression of distance. We had been near the end of the Maplins when we had found the *Atlantic*.

Another half an hour, and this could have been a very different story with a very different outcome. As we closed the shore we could see people walking out to us and I headed toward them. It was our shore crew coming to get us. We nearly got to them but we started to hit the ground so I stopped the engine and tilted the out board. The crews grabbed the boat and started to walk to the shore.

"Come on Gilson, you fat git, get out," one of them said, and they all laughed. We got over the side and they quickly went ahead of us. It was only then that we realised how much the job had taken out of us. They were pulling the boat in to the shore twice as fast as we could walk. They had been thinking ahead and had brought the trailer from the inshore shed down to the beach. With so many willing hands, hard jobs become easy and this was one of them. The boat was lifted into the trailer and pulled to the beach. I have no recollection of the ride back to the boathouse or getting the boat ready for sea. Was I tired? Or reflecting on what might have been?

I was awarded a Thanks on Vellum for this job. The citation read: "In recognition of the skill and determination displayed by him when the lifeboat went to the assistance of the Southend *Atlantic* 21 class Lifeboat "*Percy Garon*" in a south-south-westerly violent storm, steep heavy seas and total darkness in the early hours of the morning of the 21st October 1989."

I do feel that the many crew should have got a thank you because without the whole team, I could not have carried out the job. On the other hand, it was good fun. Perhaps that is reward enough?

The *Atlantic* had apparently struck the barge several times while getting a crewman on board. The crew of the barge said they were hard aground and would wait until the tide came back and they would be okay. After retrieving the crewman, the lifeboat engines had somehow stalled and would not restart and she then started to drift across the Maplins, which is where I started the story. The *Atlantic* was recovered by Roger Burrows, a farmer from Foulness Island with a very large all terrain fork lift. His was one of the families that Dad had become good friends with after meeting them during the famous floods on Foulness in 1953.

It was the only time in 30 years, that my wife said: "Be careful!" I often wonder what she was thinking about while I was gone!

*Endeavour on Strand Wharf soon after she was returned to Leigh in 2001,
with many of the people that worked on restoring her.
From left to right: Ron Myall, Peter Smith, Finlay Marshall, Peter Dolby, George Cox
(who makes lovely bread) and Peter Wexham.*

Endeavour on passage to Dunkirk, leaving the White Cliffs of Dover behind.

The Endeavour

I AM VERY FORTUNATE and privileged to be the helmsman of *Endeavour*. Originally built in 1926, she was the last wooden cockle bawley built to sail and the first to have an inline engine. She is more importantly one of "The Little Ships" of the Second World War, a Dunkirk veteran. In the next chapter, I will explain more about how when the Navy called up all sea-worthy vessels in May 1940 to help in a rescue plan of allied troops, six cockle boats left from Leigh-on-Sea, but only five returned. The *Endeavour* is the only one to return to Leigh, and only by a sheer quirk of fate. She is a rescue boat with her own epic rescue story.

In June 1940, *Endeavour* had successfully returned from Dunkirk to Chatham Dockyard in Kent - where many of the "Little Ships" were signed off. Soon after, a small warship crushed her and broke two ribs on the starboard side at the back of the cabin by the bulkhead. She was reconditioned and used for fishing in the River Thames and later the Medway, until she was wrecked in the 1987 hurricane. Little more was known about *Endeavour*'s history until 1991 when she was purchased for £1 by an enthusiast, who then spent £1,500 of his own money trying to restore her.

In 2001, she was still under restoration at the Beacons Boatyard in Rochester, Kent, when members of the trust that now owns her had gone to the boatyard. They had intended buying another Leigh cockle boat, the *Resolute,* which is also a Dunkirk veteran. The trust wanted to restore the *Resolute* as a memorial to the fishermen of Leigh who lost their lives on the *Renown,* the cockle boat which was blown up by a mine on the return journey. However, the *Resolute* was in such a state that the members of the trust thought she was beyond repair. It was then the *Endeavour* was pointed out. A deal was struck and she was soon on her way back to Leigh-on-Sea.

I had been approached by the trust's chairman, Mike King, to see if I would be interested in being part of the bid to restore *Endeavour*. I did point out that my skills were limited, as painting and carpentry were not things that I excelled at. I went to see *Endeavour* when she arrived in Leigh and was taken aback - she was a wreck! I could not see how we could ever get this heap of rotting wood even to float, let alone back to sea. However Mike was very persuasive and I joined up. A team was put together and funds were raised. Local people put in vast sums of money, donations came from businesses around the town, and we won a National Lottery grant. We were the butt of many jokes from many people in the fishing industry who thought us mad, yet we carried on. Despite setbacks, like having timber stolen and trouble finding a boat builder prepared to restore her, she was eventually rebuilt at Great Totham in Essex, where the smack, *Pioneer,* was also restored. The *Endeavour* was reunited with the sea only a week before the 65th anniversary of the Evacuation of Dunkirk in May 2005, and I was to helm her there.

Leigh-on-Sea has a rich fishing heritage. For centuries it was a small fishing village and at some stage the Gilsons have been related with all the main sea-faring dynasties: the Osbornes, Deals, Denchs, and Cotgroves, to name but a few. The Gilsons have been in Leigh since the early 1800s. Heather's family, the Joscelynes, have lived here for generations too. Around 1831, one of Heather's ancestors, John Joscelyne, was a constable of St Clement's Church, alongside one of mine, John Gilson, who was a baker. It was Joscelyne's job to ensure that Gilson was making bread for the poor to a high enough standard, after a donation was made to the church to feed the poor of Leigh.

Just over a century later, my father–in law Harold and his two brothers Sonny and Vincent volunteered to go to Dunkirk on one of the requisitioned cockle boats. They were assigned to the *Renown* but after some altercation ashore they were taken off and the *Renown's* own crew took her. Harold and Sonny instead went to war on a barge that was towed to France by one of the Sun Tugs. It is here that the Dunkirk story gets ever so very personal. How different my own life might have been if Harold had gone to war on the *Renown*.

ENDEAVOUR

The Endeavour is one of the "Little Ships"
That set out on the most arduous of trips

They left on a very grey day
To a beach a long way away

They were taking a very big chance
To get our soldiers back from France

Bombarded from land and air
They were lucky the weather was fair

Many who left were not to return
Bombed, sunk and left to burn

This boat has so much to tell
Of the men and women that fell

Rescued from a mud berth
To again plough the surf

To once more do the trip
In this little ship

No bombs or machine gun fire
A trip that we won't tire

A weekend away at the end of May
To thank God for those that got away

Paul, with Pat King's dog Bonnie, in Dunkirk,
looking over at Endeavour with her sails set.

Dunkirk Spirit

Part One

S OUTHEND FISHERMEN PLAYED a vital role in the Second World War. In May 1940, the Royal Navy called up all sea-worthy boats in England as part an evacuation plan called Operation Dynamo to rescue troops from the beaches of northern France.

Some 850 boats left UK shores for the mission, including a 700 strong flotilla of merchant marine boats, fishing boats, pleasure craft, and RNLI lifeboats, which became known as the "Dunkirk Little Ships." Because of their shallow draught, these boats could rescue soldiers from the beach and ferry them to larger boats offshore.

Six cockle boats, including The *Endeavour*, answered the call to help the evacuation, as well as many pleasure boats from Southend and Leigh. The Southend Lifeboat also went but with a naval crew, because it all happened so quickly and her own crew were not on board. They all set sail on 31st May 1940 under the control of Sub Lieutenant M H B Soloman RN. But only five cockle boats returned: The *Renown*, having done the job in France, hit a mine while under tow back in Dover. Her crew, three young fishermen and a Naval Rating, were all lost.

Endeavour is the only surviving fishing boat in Leigh that went to Dunkirk and is registered with the Association of Dunkirk Little Ships. As her skipper, I was again tasked to return the veteran cockle bawley to Dunkirk to celebrate the 70th Anniversary of the evacuation. This trip was the big one, the media had been hyping it up for weeks. This was probably going to be the last voyage for many of the surviving veterans of what is still known as "The Miracle of Dunkirk" when the "Little Ships" rescued over 300,000 British, French and Belgian troops.

As preparations were underway for her return to Dunkirk, confidence was high as we were now more used to *Endeavour*, having owned her five years by then. She is a good sea boat, but she is very wet. There is nowhere to hide, you are part of the boat and you have to take it on the chin. For this trip my crew were Peter Dolby and Finlay Marshall as well as two of the Osborne family, Graham and Trevor. Their family had owned the *Renown* and they had lost a relation in the 1940 disaster. Finally, Cameron McGregor, alias Jimbo, a fine figure of a man, our translator and a speaker of many tongues, some of which other people could understand, especially the French and Germans. Cameron and I had played rugby for many years together. I was loose-head prop and he was my second row. We knew each other intimately, he would say.

The format was the same as five years earlier: we could leave Leigh on the Tuesday with the fall back day as Wednesday for our outward trip to Ramsgate. I had been watching the changing weather forecast for over a week and it had not changed much, fresh to strong easterly for Tuesday freshening throughout the day and very fresh for Wednesday. I was not looking forward to this at all. On our first Dunkirk trip, the weather to Ramsgate was poor but as it was from the south west we could get a lee from the land and we sailed all the way to North Foreland. She flew, we achieved speeds of over 9 knots over the ground. Not bad for an old bawley. But this time it was fresh, with winds touching 30 knots. We had put some gear aboard on Monday evening so we only had to put on board water to drink, food and the bags of clothes that we had to wear once we got to Dunkirk. Now I am not one of the world's tidiest of men but I do try. When I put my blazer on board I made every effort to hang it up so it would not be creased at the many of the functions that we would be attending. As others put their gear on board they followed suit and hung their best clothes in the same place as mine. The other cases were placed in the hold and covered with a large canvas to keep them dry. The hatches were placed and covered with a canvas cover; she should then be water tight.

Tuesday 25 May 2010, Bell Wharf, Leigh-on-Sea 10.30 wind E Force 4

We left from her berth outside Osborne's cockle stall and moved down the creek to Bell Wharf. I was not hopeful and was in two minds about whether to go. Only three of the crew were there, Peter, Fin and Graham. I expressed my concern and Graham rang Trevor to say not to come down as it looked doubtful that we would go. The media and friends were starting to arrive; members of the trust were also there. If I could sail, it would steady the boat and it would be a better ride. But no, as the wind was due east I could not get an angle. If I were to tack back and forth into the wind it would take forever, so that was out. If we were to try tomorrow we would almost certainly not go, because the wind would be even stronger. If we left it until Thursday morning we would not be able to catch up and I did not fancy crossing the Channel on my own on Friday, as the weather forecast was again poor. So we had little choice but to go for it.

"Okay everybody, we will try. If it gets too bad we will drop back to Whitstable." I announced.

Graham again rang a surprised Trevor. "Change of plan. Get your butt down here, we are going to go," he said.

"Okay, be down in five," Trevor replied. True to his word he soon turned up, as did Cameron when we rang.

"Everyone must put on their life jacket and full wet weather gear. This is going to be very wet," I explained, when all were assembled. "It is not quite as windy as last time but we will be straight into the weather. Shame they forgot to put on a wheelhouse."

There were a few smiles at my joke and some nervous laughter. More pictures were taken, with press calling: "Smile, look this way, over here". I know it's important - but I was desperate to get going. I kept looking at the clock, I wanted to put to sea but there seemed so much the people wanted.

"Paul! Here, take this. It may help at some stage." David Norman, a local councillor passed a bag with just a neck of a bottle showing and gave me a knowing wink. A bottle of dark rum, for medicinal purposes no doubt, and as a dry ship I decided better put that some place safe. Everyone was dressed for the Arctic, putting on full wet weather gear. Trevor could not get his life jacket on because of what he called a crease in his jacket, Cameron managed and he had a much bigger crease. He had been growing his for years.

On our first trip to Dunkirk we managed to sail *Endeavour* to Ramsgate but not this time. The wind was right on her nose. We would have to use the engine.

Bell Wharf 11.30 wind E force 5

"Okay then let's go, let go forward, let go aft," I called to crew. Ropes came aboard and were quickly coiled up. I asked that all the fenders and ropes be put below and any loose gear put away. The hatches were re-covered with the canvas hatch cover so she should be water tight, or so I thought.

"Fin, can you check that the air vent is closed in the cabin?"

Already water was starting to splash aboard and we were still in Leigh Creek. Fin got the wrong end of the message and checked the fitting on the deck not underneath.

"It's all tight skipper," he said. I suspected then that he was wrong.

"Put the kettle on while you are up there, it may get too rough later to get a hot drink."

"I knew that was coming," he replied.

We were quickly out of the creek and then the Ray. We crossed the Sea Reach channel on the very top of the tide so although it was choppy it was not being made worse by the ebb tide.

Fin and Peter were both at the tea-making but nothing was forth coming. The rest of the boys were sitting on the starboard side of the hatch with their backs to the worst of the weather. They had a little more shelter than one would have thought with the Boom and sail keeping some of the weather off them. We were on an east-south-east course so the waves were splashing up her port side and still no tea.

"The gas bottle is empty," they said as one, coming up from the cabin. Odd, I thought, worked all right yesterday when I checked it. I explained that before it got too rough I would open the front of the hold, get out the spare gas bottle and put down the centre-plate, which is a brake to stop her rolling and then ease her down (meaning take the power off the engine).

"Will it make a difference?" Graham asked.

"It will slow her down a bit but it will keep her a bit steadier and stop her rolling too violently," I replied. They did not at this time realise just how fast and violently she could roll but within a few hours it became fully apparent.

Crossing Nore 12.45 heavy swell wind E Force 5/6

We were crossing the Nore and watching a large cargo boat coming out of the River Medway. I had time to cross in front of it and it was so big it looked much closer than it was but one must play it safe. She was probably doing 20 knots to our meagre 7. I eased her down again and went round the ship's stern. The new gas bottle was fitted but still no tea appeared.

"Cannot get it to light and the kettle is being thrown off the cooker, skipper," Peter said. "I have a bottle of water here. Will that do?" He said this grinning!

I changed course and everyone settled down, talking and drinking water. Waves hitting the port side were throwing up spray and the wind blew it across us, but this was nothing compared to what was to come. For now, we were only getting damp. We made good progress across the Spile and down towards Reculver, just east of Herne Bay. This is the site of a Roman fort used for centuries as a landmark by navigators.

The bad news was still no tea. Because of the spray we had to close the cabin so no water could penetrate from the deck. The engine room hatch was also closed, so we were water tight. After some two and a half hours at sea, I suggested that we had a sandwich and a short respite. We should check all was okay below.

"We're okay," various voices said. "We can go a bit further."

"No, you don't understand. If you do not eat now you will not be able to until much later," I pointed out There were some derogatory remarks about my parentage but they reluctantly opened the hatches and released a big bag of rolls that Graham had brought from the cockle stall. I had put *Endeavour* stern to the wind and she was sailing back up river on bare poles at three knots and out of gear.

Mouth of Gore Channel 14.15 E Force 6

The rolls were soon eaten and the surplus put away and we headed back to sea on passage to the Gore Channel. The Gore Channel is a small gap in between the sand banks where you hold deep water to get to the south of the Margate Sands. It is only a hundred metres wide but ideal for small boats like us to use. It keeps them out of the main shipping channels and you get a little shelter from the sand banks as you move down the coast. Unfortunately, the sand banks were not going to help much today as we were all but head to wind. As soon as we were through I shaped her back to the east holding, with the sand bank close on my port side, hoping that it would give us more shelter. But the wind was too straight, so there was no shelter. We also had a bit more tide here so the sea was getting livelier, more waves and bigger ones at that. I dropped the revs on the engine to reduce the speed, no need to make it worse that it already was. Nearly every wave put spray across the boat and the swells were getting bigger. Some of that spray was starting to become solid and green splashes became the norm.

SE Margate 15.30 ENE Force 6/7

We passed the SE Margate buoy and I now had to guide her around some of the bigger waves. She was now putting her nose under and green water was coming aboard and running along the decks. The boys were struggling to sit still, their hoods were covering their faces but I could hear them laughing as heavy spray and green water splashed around them. The centre-plate was now doing its job - we were rolling and pitching but less than we otherwise would. They pushed themselves back on to the hatch cover as every wave tried to push them off. I was getting covered in spray by virtually every wave, looking through my glasses was like being in a fog, I was constantly wiping them.

As we neared Margate a familiar looking coloured boat came into sight: the Margate Lifeboat. It was at this point I was very near to turning back, as I thought that this was as much sea as *Endeavour* could put up with. Yet when we passed a yacht that appeared to be make much more fuss of it than us, I thought I would give it a little longer. With the lifeboat near by and now taking pictures of us, the boys could see just how rough it was. Her hull was disappearing in the troughs and she was shearing about all over the place. I wondered what they thought of us, all but an open boat with the crew only sat on the hatches. I knew what I would be thinking. We had only another twenty minutes to go and we would be turning round the North Foreland, but I knew that could be the worst twenty minutes of the trip. I asked Fin to get the camera out and take pictures, but got a curt reply. "You must be joking? I cannot even stand, let alone take a picture."

"All right, keep your hair on, but you have to admit it would make a cracking picture," I replied. "Can anyone see a red buoy or a beacon?"

"Yes, on her nose," came the reply

"That's the Long Nose. Once round that, the wind will be on our quarter and we will be over the worst."

The lifeboat had left us and we were on our own when the biggest wave of the trip reared up in front of us. "Look at the size of that bastard!" I exclaimed. Nobody looked - they held on as I took *Endeavour* behind it. Every wave now ran along the deck but after what felt an age we rounded the fore land and were bound south.

Long Nose 16.30, ENE   Force 6/7, Heavy swell with breaking waves

For the first time in over an hour I could see clearly, my glasses were clean and *Endeavour* was riding high on some big waves that were now coming from the NE. The banter started again, it may have been happening all the time but I could not hear it. But I did hear: "Cup of tea, Skip?"

"Oh, okay, you twisted my arm, and check if there is any water down there, please."

We ran down past Broadstairs and onto Ramsgate, and at last a cup of tea came into my hand. We had made it. I checked in with the port control on the VHF and was given a berth to head for. There were already many "Little Ships" berthed in the marina, which had arrived over the weekend when it was calm.

Ramsgate Harbour 17.30 N E Force 6 Heavy swell

The first boat we berthed alongside, MTB 102, had a film crew aboard and I could see one of the presenters from the programme Coast on board. "That long haired Scotsman," was a comment I heard from our deck. We were redirected to another berth among smaller boats and quickly moored up. Gear was soon being passed out of the hold. It was then we found that the air vent that Fin had checked earlier was not water tight and our best clothes had had a wash.

"It's only water," I said. "We are here safe and sound, we can always find a dry cleaners tomorrow."

I felt like it took forever to walk up the hill from the harbour to the Royal Temple Yacht Club, with its new bar and alterations since our last visit. We had two rooms booked: one of four beds and one of two. Fortunately for the rest of us, our two professional snorers took the double. Fin and Cameron had been in the English snoring team for some time but it was a sport that had not yet taken off and they were left with just a training programme. Some wanted a beer but I needed a wash and some dry clothes. I entered our room took off my clothes and went to have a shower. I then had a bit of a shock.

Looking in the mirror I saw this white-faced man with greyish white hair looking back. I was covered in salt! I showered and dried myself and looked again. What a difference there was: now very red-faced man was looking back with very blood shot eyes! I had been burnt by the weather. This was going to hurt. I was knackered. I had been on my feet for six hours and it felt like it. The boys came up and started to get ready only to find that much of their clothing that had been in the cases in the hold was also wet. It really was not surprising considering the water that had been thrown about.

We adjourned to the bar and decided to go out to an Italian restaurant, where Cameron came into his own again as he could read the menu. I believe it was he who suggested the house wine, a very nice red and considering the selection we had over the next week we felt it the best not only for taste but value. We did try several bottles and they were all good so it was not just one good bottle.

Paul and crew enjoying a very good meal at the Italian restaurant in Ramsgate. One of several good nights out.

I believe that the trip down, the food, tiredness and the wine had started to glue us all together, and at this point Trevor made one of his profound statements. "I don't drink normally" he said, before ordering another bottle. He said we deserved it but that he would abstain, only to claim someone had filled his glass and as manners meant a lot to him, he would finish it. Oh, we did laugh. It was soon dark and fatigue was setting in. We headed back in the yacht club for a swift G&T before bed.

Ramsgate, Wednesday 26th May 2010

Next morning the weather was still blowing. At the Royal Temple you make you own breakfast so for me it was tea and toast. Today was a busy day for Ramsgate. It was their turn to pay their respects, and as we watched the breakfast news it was all about the "Little Ships". We made our way down to the boat about 8.45 am to open her up and let some air in and try to dry her off a bit.

We made a remarkable discovery. It was hard to believe, but where the boys had been sitting their feet had worn the paint off the deck. You could quite clearly see where each of them had sat; they had been pushing back so hard they had worn the paint off the deck. I then checked where I had been standing, and sure enough you could clearly see the paint had gone from under my right foot, that had been the foot doing all the work keeping me upright on our passage down. Fin, our painter and decorator, was ridiculed as he did the painting of the decks, but he put up a valiant fight not realising for some time that we were taking the mickey.

While we were interrogating Fin on his painting prowess, I was approached by another skipper asking if I could move *Endeavour* to let his boat in. At first I was reluctant, as it was very windy and it would be very hard holding her in the middle of the marina and letting the other boat in. However, after he explained that the boat was called *Amazon* and was 75 feet long, I agreed to move. She was one of the nicest looking boats of her time, long and sleek, class. He brought her in and made a very professional job of putting her alongside. There again, he had a bow thruster and twin screws, making her easier to manoeuvre. He also had two very small crew, who were exceptionally nimble about the deck with fenders and ropes. This crew were so good my crew started to loose concentration and became crew watchers. I could not blame them, for it was two young women, probably Thai or possibly Filipino girls who were crewing this boat, and seemed to bending down a lot to tie the fenders up - well, boys will be boys!

We moored back alongside this beautiful boat,trying with our one propeller to make an equally professional job, and I think we did. I did wonder what attracted that kind of crew to a probable multimillionaire owner of a luxury yacht when they could have been on *Endeavour*. I looked at Fin and Cameron, and well, their expressions said it all.

After a second breakfast in a café, we walked the short distance to the church where there were many people hanging about. Peter and I made a quick decision, to go in and get a seat. The church had atmosphere, not cold but welcoming, and we took our seat in a rapidly filling room. We were given an order of service booklet, and on opening it, the name The Rev Peter Tizzard stuck out like a sore thumb. Tizzard is a name that fascinates me; we have a sand bank in the Thames called the Tizzard Bank where I have had many good fishing trips over the years. It was called the Tizzard, supposedly after Commander Tizzard who surveyed the Thames in the 1800 - a nice story, true or not. Within no time the church was full and people were standing, the centre aisle filled with the standards of many groups and organisations, the bearers wearing medals that probably only see day light a couple of times a years sparkling on their chests.

The service began with the Rev Tizzard welcoming us and the reasons for being there. We sang a good hymn to start: "O God our help in ages past." A prayer, then the lesson, followed by old faithful "Eternal Father Strong to Save." A large lump always comes to my throat when singing this song and today was no different. It was actually one of many occasions over the next few days when emotions stopped me talking and struck me dumb. Another prayer, then the Exhortation: "They shall grow not old, as we that are left grow old. Age shall not weary them, nor the years condemn. At the going down of the sun and in the morning we will remember them."

We replied as one: "We will remember them." The "Last Post" was played by a group of buglers, which just about finished me off. Thankfully, they then played Reveille. The epitaph followed: "When you go home tell them of us and say for your tomorrow we gave our today." The standards withdrew and we followed them out and thanked the vicar for an emotional service. Outside, we quietly formed up to watch the parade file past.

It was then I met John Hoskins, a Little Ship owner, and we were soon chatting away. He had brought his boat down by trailer from the depths of darkest Leicestershire and had only launched her the previous day. The parade finished and we wandered off to have a couple of hours to ourselves before the Mayor of Ramsgate's reception later in the afternoon.

I was more fortunate than my crew. They went sightseeing to a bar while I met some good friends with whom I had a long-running invitation to a sauna, jacuzzi and then lunch. I had a very very pleasant afternoon that passed much too quickly. With only minutes to spare I was back at the yacht club, changed and again back in my official role as the Helmsman of *Endeavour*. With Trevor in tow, we were again off to an official engagement at the Old Customs House, the new residence of the Mayor of Ramsgate. We were cordially invited in to be introduced to the mayor and offered some wine by two young women dressed as 1940s waitresses. Trevor was very quick to point out that he felt they were showing much too much cleavage for the era. I pointed out that like his thoughts the costumes may well have come from a shop specialising in fantasy.

We found ourselves with John again and were quickly talking of what lay ahead tomorrow. John was worried that he may have to withdraw as he had been let down by his crew and was now on his own. I felt sure that with the very large numbers of followers we could find him a crew. I had someone in mind, never realising how much that they would have in common. John was being distracted by the waitresses and obviously shopped at the same department store as Trevor. I thought at one stage we would have to hose them down or at least set the sprinklers off as they became more hot and bothered when being offered more wine. After some very nice speeches we were again watching the Ramsgate sea cadets playing hits from the 1940s in the road outside Custom House. They were very good. They had paraded past, then it was time for a briefing in the church on the next day's agenda.

As we entered, I recognized some old faces from previous rallies. Faces recognised, names forgotten, but friends nevertheless. We were quickly ushered into our pews again and a briefing ensued. Banter between groups of boats and skippers was frowned upon as we were introduced to the Officers of the Royal Navy who would be our escorts and general minders for the convoy over. The thought that was rushing through my mind was: "Aren't the officers of the Royal Navy so very young?" Bit like policemen I suppose. We received our orders, placements in the convoy, and yes, we were with the *Ferry Nymph* again - deep joy. There would be good banter between us.

The *Ferry Nymph* was the ferry in Yarmouth when her crew and that of her sister ship had answered the call and gone to Dunkirk. I first saw her in a boatyard in Leigh, where she was being converted to a trawler. She was totally unsuited for this role and she became a common casualty for the RNLI.

She was renamed the *Sheppard Lad*, and the Sheerness lifeboat attended her five, if not six times and the Southend Lifeboat many more. I was called to her aid twice. Once, in a force 10, when every effort was made to save her, but she still sank even after we had put a large salvage pump aboard in horrendous conditions. We got her to shallow and sheltered water all to no avail - she still sank. The owner then allegedly threatened the RNLI with court action for not doing enough to save his boat. We saved his life, so you would have thought that would have been good enough, but as I have found on several occasions, often it is not. A new owner had brought her and restored her to her original condition. She is now sleek and fast and he is a very proud owner.

At the briefing, we were informed about our Naval cadet who would be coming with us. It was just as in the original operation, when a navy rating was assigned on every vessel. We were instructed no alcohol was to be given to the cadet at all - I bet that did not happen the first time! We also met the pilot of the Hurricane that was to give us a fly past, he also made me feel old.

The aircraft was based at what was RAF Manston for this weekend and he would be flying over us several times. He explained that he had only a compass to navigate with and things were very basic. It was so interesting to learn that he was restricted to flying only in dry weather, as if it was wet the wooden propeller wears out to quickly and they do not have many replacements. Another problem was the airfields. The Hurricane was designed to take off from a grass field. Manston had a runway and if the wind was not in the correct direction, he was not allowed to attempt take off. We could have chatted to him for the rest of the day but he was whisked off to talk to someone else.

I was left in no doubt that he loved what he was doing and enjoyed ever minute of his life. Our instructions were to join the slow group to leave berth at 6 am as we could not do more than seven knots under motor, while the fast group would leave last, catch up in mid-channel then rush on ahead to berth first in Dunkirk. We were then briefed on the trip to Wormhout, but to our horror we had not got a place booked and the coaches were full.

Ramsgate Thursday 27th May 2010

We woke at 5.15 am, tea was made and a peek outside revealed dreary rain and grey skies but no wind. The banter started again on who was snoring the loudest and the most, depending on who was doing the accusing. We must all be snorers or liars or both. We put on full sailing gear just for the short walk down to the *Endeavour*.

Standing at the top of the hill looking over the harbour, my mind wondered what it must have looked like that morning 70 years ago, with literally thousands of men being deposited on the quay side and hundreds of small and large boats coming in and out. There was no radio guidance to tell them what and where to go, yet they managed. The NAFFI canteens on the quay side with tea and cigarettes. But who organised the food, the medical staff? How do you get so much stuff moved at such short notice? Could we do it now? How would health and safety cope with it? The first thing is that the boats used then would not be deemed sea-worthy now: no life saving gear, surveys, nor tests on competency. What about a risk assessment? It does not bear too much thinking about. We simply could not do it now.

Cameron waved us goodbye as he went of to crew for John. We arrived at *Endeavour* to find Josh, our Navy cadet, already there. We welcomed him aboard and gave him the house rules: life jackets at all times and no alcohol, but copious amounts of tea were permitted. The VHF was soon crackling into life with our Commodore telling us that all was okay (actually it was not; the Commodore's vessel was aground but we only learnt this later in the week.) The weather was good, so we formed up outside the harbour into our groups. I was watching the chaos that was starting to develop around the marina as different boats got under way at the same time. The *Endeavour* has many faults but a quick get away is not one of them, the engine was started and ropes released and we were outside the harbour in under five minutes. The quay side was full of well-wishers even at this time in the morning, flags were flying, horns rang out and people waved. It was very moving. I felt humble and proud all at the same time. It was funny: on Tuesday we needed a wheelhouse to escape the weather, but today we had the advantage of not having one, giving us all-round visibility.

"Kettle's on, skip," Peter said. He was doing well. While we were out enjoying the previous day, he had been shopping, getting bacon and rolls for the trip over. He felt that he had been domesticated from having been retired some years, bless him. I was very pleased we got out when we did as it took some boats a long time to get on station, but within an hour we were formed up and on our way.

The media was everywhere: planes, boats and helicopters, filming everything that was going on. As we cleared the Ramsgate Channel we were soon doing 7 knots and it looked like this would be a faster trip than last time. The fast Navy patrol boat, *HMS Raider*, was leading us and in the distance we could see *HMS Monmouth*, The Black Duke to her friends, the only ship that can fly a black flag apparently. The sea had calmed down but there was an occasional swell rolling through from the previous day's strong winds. A good cup of tea was produced from the cabin and permission was sought to cook some breakfast, with permission duly granted. The rain and drizzle had stopped but it was still cold so when the bacon butties arrived all was put right. I had brought with me suntan cream but having been burnt so much the first day and with no sun at all today I felt it was a waste of time. After our rolls and tea the atmosphere on the boat was very good. All were enjoying the ride and the banter. We were soon down off Dover and turning to cross the main shipping lane, the fast group caught us up and we crossed the lane at right angles.

I can only wonder what it must have looked like on the radar screens at Dover as they tracked our armada of vessels crossing the busiest shipping lane in the world. There was some concern as a very large container ship closed in on the fleet but we need not have worried. We had The *Anglian Monarch*, a large rescue tug, join us. She was like a babysitter or teacher's assistant, there to reassure us and keep away the bad guys. She was actually there to represent the Sun Tugs that took part in the evacuation, a company that had been taken over by The *Anglian Monarch's* owners.

More tea was made and drunk. Keeping station was not too difficult this time. On our previous trip, we were continually taking the boat out of gear because the convoy was so slow. We were soon in French waters and were greeted by their version of the RNLI. I do like the look of the French boats, sleeker than our boats and a nice shade of green. Fin and Graham both had a spell at the helm but neither felt at home in their role and I soon had it back.

The French coast was soon on our starboard side and we were going north-north-east a few miles off the coast. The fast group had detached itself from us so they could get locked into Dunkirk before the slow group got there. As we found last time, getting in and out the lock took time, with several bumps and shunts. The fast boats soon disappeared over the horizon and we looked at the industrial coast line of Northern France. Not a sight to inspire poetry or romantic verse, but never the less it was there. Having passed Gravelines, the large modern port, we could see Dunkirk coming up and our fast boats were nearly all in. Other than one old boat over-heating we had made it unscathed. The media again was here with helicopters whirling around us and the French lifeboats had cameras on board. Was nowhere safe? Ropes and fenders were positioned and made ready. We soon entered the harbour taking in the very long arm or Mole that so many soldiers escaped from. The Mole was in fact a long breakwater that stretched out into deeper water allowing access to the evacuating boats for a longer period of time than the beaches. We were to wait in the outer harbour until called so we could be berthed in the lock in some order.

The harbour at Dunkirk is vast, it is the biggest harbour I have ever been in and the water is kept at a set depth. This allows vessels with a deep draught to avoid touching the bottom when the tide goes out and makes for easy unloading. To keep the water at this level there are two huge locks that act as lifts and stoppers. They keep the water in and allow ships in at most states of the tide too, the ship would enter the lock and a gate closed behind it. The water would be drained down from the main harbour to fill the lock to the same height as the harbour then another gate would open and the ship would pass out of the lock into the main harbour.

A tight squeeze in Dunkirk Harbour.

It should be so simple, but last time we were here it was not, many of our colleagues were just not used to working in close proximity to one another. Boats rammed each other and tempers became quite stretched, one beautiful boat that had been kept in a glass case all year was what we call "t-boned" or rammed mid-ship with a very loud crash. Others had bumps and shunts. I was not going to be part of that with *Endeavour*. People forget it's not a car but a boat and needs room to manoeuvre, it is actually the stern that moves. We were called and given our position alongside one of the London pleasure boats. I was going to do this differently. It would be perfect and the Navy was going to be driving. As we entered the outer harbour, Josh had the helm and he was just like on autopilot. I would let him helm the boat into the dock, and as we entered the lock, the media was there in force. On every vantage point there was a camera. If we got this wrong it would be seen worldwide. as *Endeavour*, with her bright green colour, is very distinctive. She was in many media shots over the next few days and here we were in the middle of the lock in pride of place, I felt.

"Okay Josh, you are going to put her alongside, just do as I tell you and make sure you are dressed correctly. Your mum and the Navy will be watching you. Trust me, I know how this works."

He adjusted his hat and just said: "Okay."

I bet he was very nervous. We had positioned *Endeavour* I felt perfectly, with everyone in place on time with fenders and ropes in case of the unexpected. With no fuss at all we went alongside. If I were to be critical we touched six inches too early, and that was my fault for going in reverse too early, but to the outsider it was perfect. Ropes were passed and we quickly moored up.

"Well done young man," I said to Josh. I don't know how he felt but the smile that broke out on his face was worth the whole trip.

"Have you ever done anything like that before?" I asked.

"Never," he replied.

Another half an hour and I could relax. I was not counting on interference from the crew of *Ferry Nymph*, who offered us a beer to drink onboard *Endeavour*. Knowing full well that we were a dry ship, my crew was looking aft with pleading eyes. I pointed to the boat we were moored alongside.

"Just pop aboard the next boat for a bit," I said to my crew who gave me some very puzzled looks. "Because they are not a dry ship."

They quickly caught on and there was much laughter from Jonathan and his crew as we relieved them of five cans of cold beer. Poor Josh was not allowed one but I think he was still enjoying his moment.

The water level climbed quickly and the lock was soon open. A procession made its way through the docks to the inner dock area where we would moor and be on display. The mooring master had made a good job of getting us all through in an orderly and disciplined operation.

A ferry from Dover had entered by the other sea lock, her upper deck was loaded with veterans. We could see a great many standards being held on deck and hundreds of people cheering us waving flags as we slipped by.

The next dock would contain all the war ships once they had passed through the lock, there was a Belgium war ship already there. I think her name was *Stern* or *Star*, but my Flemish is not that good. Into the penultimate dock, we passed an old English paddle steamer and numerous yachts moored to the quay side all waving and carrying flags.

A hard turn to port placed us in the inner dock, right in the middle of the town. Ahead of us, dressed all over with bunting was a tall ship with three masts, the *Duchesse Anna*, and on our starboard side the modern civic centre, a mixture of old and new.

It was going to be a great experience.

Old Soldier's Story

WITH MY CONNECTIONS with the *Endeavour* and the Association of Dunkirk Little Ships (ADLS) I have met some very interesting old soldiers at different events. This particular poem is based on a veteran corporal I met at a Ramsgate rally in May of 2011. He was aged about 90 and was in a wheelchair but could stand with a little help. His story went like this:

"I was sent across to Dunkirk when the evacuation had already started, my unit was to go to the front and form part of a rear guard strategy. We were given some time in Dunkirk before we were sent to the front, so my mates and I went to a brothel before we marched to our positions.

"We were given 60 rounds each as we took up positions along a canal bank and told to hang on to the last. The officer wished us good luck and he moved on. By the morning we had run out of ammunition and there were only three of us left. The Germans were already across the canal and on either side of us. We felt we had done our best and would head for the beach. I got on the last ship from the Mole, my mates did not make it."

I believe when he was talking to me, he was back there re-living it with his mates, now ghosts but still his companions.

The Old Soldier

60 rounds he was given
Then marched to the front
60 rounds he was given
The enemy to confront

60 rounds he was given
To keep the Hun at bay
60 rounds he was given
To last throughout the day

60 rounds he was given
It could be hand-to-hand
60 rounds he was given
This could be his last stand

60 rounds he was given
He used them through the night
60 rounds he was given
Germans on the left and right

60 rounds they'd been given
The platoon had done its best
60 rounds he'd been given
His mate took one in the chest

The Old Soldier

60 rounds they had all been given
But like the rounds they were all gone
60 rounds they had all been given
It had gone so very wrong

60 rounds all empty
Lay around his feet
60 rounds all spent
As he crawled along the street

60 rounds none wasted
He did not want to die
60 rounds all gone
He had no time to think of why

60 rounds meant nothing
As he headed back to the coast
60 rounds meant nothing
He had now a ghost

60 rounds he told me
Oh he done us proud
60 rounds I heard him say
As he was wheeled back into the crowd

A bountiful catch of cod.

Cod Fishing in The Thames

IT WILL PROBABLY be a surprise to you to know that for many years the Thames Estuary area was a top area for cod. The prime spot for cod-fishing was where the water became deeper and did not dry out at the edge, and most cod were found around Blyth Sands, a large area of sand and mud stretching from the mouth of the River Medway almost to Gravesend, and from the shore to the main channel on the south side of the Thames opposite Canvey Island. When I first left school in the late 1960s, we would visit the Blyth Sands in the autumn to do "the high water," a tow up and down near the East Blyth buoy. The reason it was so good was the prolific shoals of shrimp that could be found here, these shrimp had been here for hundreds of years and been fished for generations. Cod love shrimp as do whiting, and very large hauls of both these fish could be caught here.

Historically, Gravesend and Leigh-on-Sea were shrimping and whitebait ports, with well over a hundred boats in operation. Indeed both species were caught further up river, and were very popular in Victorian times, when festivals for whitebait were held at Southend and whitebait suppers served at Greenwich at the Trafalgar pub. The traditional whitebait ceremony still takes place in Southend, and I will talk more about whitebait in another chapter.

The shrimp appeared to flourish on the nutrient-rich water that could be found here or in the polluted water that came down from London. (We have learnt since that the contraceptive pill turns nine out of ten shrimp to males!) When new sewage systems were introduced in London, shrimp and whitebait declined to levels of near extinction. While it was there, though, it was a bonanza and when the railway came to Leigh-on-Sea, the shrimp could be in London the next day cooked in the water it was caught from with a handful of salt to give it a longer shelf-life.

While we were fishing, we had no idea of the bigger picture that was slowly forming which would transform our fishing and even our way of life. As a sixteen-year-old, all I wanted was to catch loads of cod and have enough money to take my girlfriend out to the pictures and then a Chinese at the Good Will Restaurant on a Saturday night.

On this particular day we were fishing with the *Ros Beara*, towing a Larsen trawl, which is just a very square and long net towed between two boats. The *Ros Beara* was the bigger boat and the net was shot from her stern deck. There were four corners called wings (two per boat: one top, one bottom), with a large sinker or weight attached to the end of the bottom warp and the net attached by cliphook or G-link to the wire as well. This would open the net up and down and the two boats hold it open so making a square. Very basic, but it worked, and at that time well. The power of the two boats was not great - 84hp for the *Paul Peter* and 150hp for the *Ros Beara*. I would go on to skipper the *Ros Beara* for several years, but by then she was well past her sell-by date.

Because we did not have the power to tow fast we had to use the tide to its best advantage, which is why we would do the high water. We could go up and down and cover more ground while the tide was slack. We turned out as soon as the tide hit the beach and as soon as there was enough water we would drag the motorboat to the slipway. We would fill them with wooden boxes, which would often be stinking because they had not been washed after the last time they had been used. We had a mooring on the shore, while the *Ros Beara* and *Hazel* - the family's other big boat, - were both moored in the Ray. It was possibly the only time the bigger boats had the advantage of being at sea first or being nearer to the fishing grounds. We unloaded boxes on our sister ship, the *Three Sons*, which was paired with the *Hazel*, and then we went out to our mooring, the furthest one out on the east of the pier.

Boxes were put aboard as well as five tins of diesel for the day. While Dad started the engine it was my job to put the kettle on and stick the juice (i.e. diesel) to one side. As soon as we were running we would make the skiff fast on the mooring and let go. The *Black Gang*, the name we gave our little boats, were close behind and we would all head out towards the pier head, six boats, three teams all going to the same place.

Tea was made for Dad as soon as possible (it kept him in a good mood).

I hated tea then, and just could not understand why so many people drank the stuff, but by the time I was in my thirties I loved the stuff! I would try and get the coal fire burning before we got shot as this would warm the cabin and keep the kettle hot for Dad and make it nice and warm for me to sleep when we were towing. Boxes were washed and stowed in to the hold as quick as I could go as it was often splashy steaming up river, and they were still made of wood then. It was usual to steam across the dump grounds on our way to the Blyth and there were always many marks on the echo sounder or fish finder. The sea bed there was at that time very rough. Dad would comment that he would love to shoot the nets here but it was thought madness because of the rubbish that lay there on the sea bed. It would be many years before I could get Dad to work there and that was only after I had been working the area with my own boat for several years. Yes, there was some good fishing to be had there - but only after I had cleared most of the moveable rubbish.

The *Black Gang* would go straight across and shoot up with the tide from the Jenkin buoy or to us at the Yantlet buoy. The other pair would go to the top end of the ground and shoot down and we would shoot up from just below the East Blyth buoy thereby not crowding or being too close. We shot with no problem and in no time I had another tea in Dad's hand and I was in my bunk rapped up in a nice warm blanket. The *Paul Peter's* engine was aft so it was nice and snug in my cabin. The downside was you could hear everything that was being said on the radio so I would get a running commentary of what was happening. They would try and tow where the best fish marks could be seen and we would go up and down and around the East Blyth Buoy until the ebb started to slow us down. I remember the comments of very good marks and at regular intervals as I dosed in my nice warm bunk.

When it came to hauling time another tea would be asked for and a "come on, get yourself ready" call from Dad. He knew it was so difficult going on deck into that cold wet place from that nice warm cosy bunk that I had been in for nearly three hours, but I did manage it. We came together and ropes were passed back and forth, the boats were heading up into the early ebb and as soon as the winches were put in gear we started to go backwards. The other teams were doing the same. Soon the sinkers were up and we gave the boats a blast ahead to wash the fish down and then a blast astern so we could pull the net in. If it was windy we would have someone at the engine controls to keep checking the boats astern and keep the weight off the gear. When the weather was fine all four of us would pull the net in, each taking a wing, top wings on the outside and bottom in the middle. As soon as the weight came off the gear, we could see we had a good haul, the sleeve was afloat and you could see large lumps floating in it and they were splashing. By the time we had the gear alongside we could see many large cod and whiting. It was the cod that caught the eye as they were large, with some over four feet long. The excitement was very infectious, laughter and banter abounded and when the first bag was opened we had an attack of silliness. Look at the size of that one and that as we pointed to this fish and that.

"Paul, get on the other deck and gut the big fish as we throw them across," said Dad.

Now this had never happened before, to start gutting before we had cleared the deck, but no problem, I told myself. Except there was a problem, as my normal knife was not up to the job, so I was quickly told to get and use the skate knife. This knife was like a shorter carving knife that we used to cut the wings off skate and remove the back bone and cut out the cheeks. A pen knife was not up to this job so this bigger, more robust knife was used - but I had never used it for cod before.

I soon got in the swing of it; these beautiful fish were being flung across the hatches to the pound in front of me. It was magic, as more fish were hoisted aboard I tried to get ahead. The starboard deck was half full and I had two more bags to come. More fish was coming across at me and I was being told to go faster and not to worry about what they were doing. I was quick but if I had gone any faster a finger would certainly have come off. I am still not sure even after all these years if they were being serious or not but I was being egged on to get done as fast as I could.

When the last bag came aboard, the *Ros Beara* was put in gear and she was turned to the east and the throttle pushed down, I realised we were not going home but down the tow, and we were going to shoot again! With only two of us on deck the cod were not coming across as fast as before but some of the fish must have weighed close to 30 pounds. I can still feel those fish as I tried to hold them still so I could slip the knife in without removing one of my own digits. Some had some fabulous roes - they looked just like a pair of shorts with the legs tied up. With many whiting being picked up on the other deck and me slashing away getting a good splattering of guts and blood, this was such good fun. Because the fish in that haul were so big, it was not taking me that long to get gutted up, so we had about three quarters of an hour to get clear. I would have the cod done but not the whiting - that would take several hours with two of us doing it. The pleasure of having a big boat was now so apparent: when you catch lots of fish, you need room to work.

Thames Cod.

I had finished the cod before it was time to shoot again. It was the fastest I believe I have ever gutted. My fingers were white and between them dried blood and guts stuck around the knuckles and on to the back of my hands, which were a little crusty. I was told to help clean down the working deck because Dad had to get back on his own boat The *Paul Peter* and put her in gear so we would go a bit faster while still tied together.

Dad made some comment about the state I was in, and to get myself washed down. I had only looked at my hands before, and could see now my oilskins were covered in blood and guts from kneeling in fish for nearly an hour, but I was done. That was the fun part - now we had twenty boxes of the whiting to gut. From gutting fish of many pounds down to cleaning fish weighing half a pound was not so glorious. Boring was what I would call it, but it had to be done. We started to slow and the boats were turned around head to tide, ready to shoot again.

The gear was soon in the water. Dad would be on his own as I had to stay on the *Ros Beara* to keep gutting and we still had to box up the cod. The boats were soon parted up and wire shot away, a slow tow up in to the tide started, when we had settled I saw Dad disappear, he had put the kettle on. We could hear the radio crackling away. Every pair had done well, the *Hazel* and *Three Sons* possibly had a bit more than us, and the little boats a bit less. Still, several tons between us, and discussions were taking place what to do for the best: we would land at the pier and send the fish ashore by train. Because we had so much fish we would not have as long a tow as normal, just long enough to break the back of the catch we had. After all, we could do only so much. After about an hour there was a tap on the wheelhouse window and a plate of bacon sandwiches was being offered.

We did not need a second tap, hands were washed and a quick snack was very welcome. No sooner had we had eaten them there was another tap and several slices of ginger cake were on offer. I fell in love with Jamaican ginger cake from Marks and Spencer's - we are still a couple but we don't meet as often as I would like.

With fresh vigour we set about getting on top of our task, although because the cod was of a good grade, washing and boxing up did not take long. The whiting were a different matter. We must have been nearly two hours into the tow when a "get washed up" signal came from the wheelhouse. We cleaned down as best we could and cleared the working deck ready to take another hopefully good haul. Because we had been towing close to the edge of the sands Dad came to us to haul, as we did not want to get ashore at this stage of the proceedings. The boats were soon tied alongside and we started to haul, the winches were very slow and not as powerful as we have now. We could see straight away we had a good catch as the net was at boiling point with the weight of fish in the end. Once the boats had been taken out of gear the net was pulled in by hand. The weight was too much for us to pull so the boats had to be put in astern to take the weight off the net and allow us to pull in the slack.

The other crewman was getting carried away and was pulling his side up too quickly and he got told off. This was not unusual when we got excited and it still happens today when you have a youngster on board. They need to get to the cod end as soon as they can to see what is in there. As the gear came closer it was obvious that he would not be disappointed. You could see the lumps in the sleeve telling us there were some very big cod and of course the whiting, loads of whiting. The sleeve was in fact white with fish, if only we had camera then to capture this bounty. Four bags of fish were hoisted aboard, not as good as the first tow but still very good. The net was pulled back on to the stern and we set about getting picked up again. Dad put his boat in gear and the skipper of the *Ros Beara* put her in gear and he took charge of both boats, heading to the Southend pier. The other boats were already on their way, the smaller boats were soon alongside but the other team stopped off the pier head and cleaned down before going alongside.

Once we were all alongside things were very busy, the older hands gutted while us youngsters carted the fish up and down the slipway. We made stacks of fish at the top of the slip and the pier staff put it on their small electric buggies, transporting it to the south station. At the station it was put on the boggy - a flat top train with a small cab and long flat back for transporting cargoes up and down the pier.

This was not a new thing - it had been going on for years - but I dread to think what health and safety would have done now with all that was going on. The thought of driving these little buggies laden with fish amongst the general public who all wanted to look into every box of fish makes me shiver now but then it was not a problem. Just imagine the scene at the north station with the public coming onto the pier and met with boxes of cod and whiting coming the other way. Yet no one batted an eyelid over it. Now you would have complaints about the hygiene and safety let alone the smell that it would leave. Everyone had a job and they did what had to be done, I think we have lost that work ethic.

The same procedure took place at the shore end of the pier, where all the extra staff or helpers came from I have no idea, but it all worked. I never actually loaded the shore end, but it was weighed, iced and then boxed ready to go to market the next day. It was only covered in a canvas sheet but we never had a complaint about poor quality fish, ever. The two big boats left the pier and went back to their moorings in the Ray and the rest of us waited for the tide to come and let us back on the shore to our moorings. I remember the concern over boxes as we had used everything we had, and were left with nothing to take to sea the next day, but we did go the next day using a very mixed bag of boxes. We pressed into service some old tin baths and sectioned off some of the deck, hoping that new boxes would come back with the lorry.

The fish would be sent all the way to Grimsby and sold on the fish market there. We sent two lorries, one of five ton and the other could carry seven tons. I cannot recall how much actually was sent that day but it had to be about nine tons of fish from the six boats.

Nowadays, that would be something like ten percent of the total allowable catch for the whole of the southern North Sea for the year for our class of boats. I cannot see this happening again in the foreseeable future, as there is so little food to support the bigger predator like cod.

I was very lucky to witness so many days like this in my early years of fishing. When I tell people that the best cod fishing you have seen was near Canvey Island they give me that funny look that says: "Is that another fisherman's story?"

Well it did happen, and it was such good fun.

Cod

I am Britain's favourite fish
The one and only national dish
Not always covered in batter
Baked or boiled it does not matter

The fishermen call me green
For many I have never been seen
You serve up my many fingers
But the smell often lingers

You are told I am in decline
But fishermen have to pay a fine
For not throwing me back
It is for quota that they lack

My numbers are really quite high
You may well give a sigh
A fisherman would say that
So as not to throw me back

Cod

The EU sets the total allowable catch.
But the figures really don't match
Destroy the fleet is the aim
Conservation the name of the game

When the UK fleet has gone
The EU will have won
My numbers will suddenly rise
Oh well that's a surprise

No boats left in the UK
So then the long plan comes into play
Other countries with fleets will chase me again
The favourite will probably be Spain

So it's politics not conservation that decides my fate
And you have all taken the bait
While I still feed the birds and seals
The EU does more shady deals

Love at first sight!
The Janeen in Clogherhead Harbour, County Louth, Ireland.

Buying a Boat in Ireland

This is different in the sense that we don't go to sea

I HAD OWNED THE *Marco Polo* for a number of years. She was a beam trawler, and we had done well with her but we were getting aggravation from the Marine Safety Agency (MSA), an organisation set up to reduce the fishing fleet in the UK, under the guise of safety. These people don't seem to have noticed though that after 20 years, the losses to fishing vessels and fishermen are just the same as when they started. An example of their mentality was when I met a radio surveyor, whose claim to fame was that he stopped the QE2 going to sea because the radio operator had not got his licence with him when they did a spot check. Another surveyor had a thing about a porthole I have, it is 5 feet above the deck, the seal is not perfect and I was told to change it as it could hamper the safety of the vessel. If water was at that level the rest of the boat would be under by as much as ten feet, so a dribble from a porthole would be irrelevant. One of my relatives summed these people up as "jobs-worths." How could you argue with that?

Another fishing method, the twin or triple rig, was gradually being adopted by the fishing industry. The idea was two or three small nets towed with the normal size doors for a boat of its size but with more ground cover and less drag from the netting. If you worked three 8-fathom nets, you would cover more sea bed than a 24-fathom net and the volume of materials would be substantially less. This should give more fish for less costs. Tommy Thomas was the probable instigator and major developer of this method. When I told him what I was looking to buy another another boat he asked had I got a good crew.

"Yes, I have one of the best. I have Tim."

"You will need it because when you find fish you will catch a lot."

We were both right. Tim was a very good crew and we caught a lot of fish. I had been saving hard for another boat, so no holidays or wasteful stuff like fast cars. I would never be able to afford a new boat, so it would have to be second hand, and there was no internet then, just the Fishing News, our trade paper. It carried a large section in the back pages of boats for sale. One day an ad stuck out. It advertised a prawn trawler, 15 meters with a 235 hp Caterpillar engine, and she was 18 years old. There was a picture, and as they say it was love at first sight. I made several phone calls and went to see Dad to get his opinion. Within the week, we were booking flights to Dublin from Heathrow. There would be four of us going: Dad, Ken Knapp, Les Telford and me. We drove to the airport at 4.30 am and parked up. We were on the 6 am flight and then the laughter and fun started, but only for us. When we were booking the flight for Sunday the 8th of November 1987, we did not know what would happen that day.

We had a sort of breakfast at the airport that to say the least was crap. I could eat almost anything but this was dreadful. We were quickly on the plane and seated when Gerry Adams, the alleged IRA supporter and President of Sinn Féin, came on to the aircraft. If it was not him, it was his double! I am not sure if it was or was not him, but it sure kept the flight quiet. We took off on time, the first flight out, as I recall. We were well entertained by a pretty, small but well proportioned stewardess. She was heavily accented with what I call a delightful Irishness and she had selected Dad for her charms. "So," she said. "You'll be here for some fishing? I can a see yees in the wellies."

Dad, bless him, was quite chuffed. "I am a fisherman but I do it with nets. We are coming over to see a fishing boat that is for sale with the view to buying it." In my opinion, Dad had pulled. She went out of her way to be nice and engage in conversation with him for most of the flight. This was not missed by me and he was ribbed several times over the day.

Once we had landed we picked up our hire car and headed for the coast. This is where we got our first real introduction to Ireland, on a dual carriageway leading north of Dublin. A man was selling newspapers. If that sounds fine, I might add he was standing on the edge of the fast lane. The scary bit is people were slowing and stopping to buy his newspapers on their way to work. No one appeared to notice nor complain about it, not even a car horn was heard, it was the norm! When we got to Drogheda, the road signs became very confusing. We saw no sign to Clogherhead our destination, so reluctantly we asked a pedestrian directions. I got out of the car and asked him the way to Clogherhead. He grabbed my arm and said. "You're on the right road, you go down there and then right follow it until you get to a church, and then left."

"Thank you," I replied, but before I had stopped speaking, he went on. "But you cannot go that way because they are one-way streets and no entries," he explained, still holding my arm. I was confused! "You need to go straight on then left and left again, follow the road until the bridge and straight on. Now when I say straight on, bear in mind the road bears to the left and right and then over the bridge." He then asked: "Where are you going?"

"We are going to look at a fishing boat we are interested in buying."

"Oh, that's okay then. Drive over there, left and right and follow the road it will be quicker that way." He released my arm and bid us a safe journey, I got back in the car and we drove off.

Once we were on the move we started to laugh what was that all about why so many routes. "Go straight on and bear in mind the road bears to the left and right," came from the back seats. We carried on along the directed route and there was no opportunity to go any way except over the bridge, all very odd. We noticed the number of people going to church - they were queuing to get in - and how bad the roads were, not much better that farm tracks. These were two things unrelated but we just don't see such things in England. Of course this was all to change in years to come when the EU flooded Ireland with money.

At last, we started to see signs to Clogherhead. Yet when we found the village, the harbour was not obvious. We did find the lifeboat station but no harbour. Confused again, we stopped alongside a teenager. I lowered the window and asked directions. He was very articulate and pointed this way and that; while he was speaking a very small dog took an interest in Dad. It was no bigger than a large guinea pig, but it growled and spat at him. It was trying desperately, jumping up at the window, to get at him. I on the other side of the car was totally lost. I had no idea what this young man was saying. It was fluent nonsense.

We drove on and then stopped and laughed again .What on earth was all that about? We had found the village idiot was our view and as for the dog, well he possibly just did not like Englishmen. This did not help us looking for the harbour; the lifeboat was on the other side of the headland. We thought, therefore, if we kept to the other side we should find it. We saw a small sign that said slipway - having not seen any thing else we went for it. It was a narrow lane and then there it was: a huge harbour, which in its prime it would have held 60 or 70 boats but now it was nearly empty.

We drove down to the quay side and it was obvious the boat that we came to see was alongside in a small inner harbour. We got out of the car and walked over to the boat. It was love at first sight.

Ken spoke first: "Not much to decide on you have got to have it."

The owner tuned up as we stared down on her from the quay side. He introduced himself and asked had we heard any news?

"What news?" we asked.

"Oh something's going on."

"Oh, we have not heard anything." We did not know then, but a huge bomb had just gone off in Enniskillen, a town in Northern Ireland, killing 11 people at a Remembrance Day ceremony.

The boat was just what we wanted. We went all over her looking for any fault that we could find. She appeared perfect. Her cabin was luxurious, with six berths, a huge diesel fire and fresh water on tap. A crane on the after-deck and a sound winch, all adding up to what we wanted. All her paperwork appeared in order and I had an English fishing licence lined up back home. Unfortunately we could not give her a test run because not only was there a gale blowing but the tides were at the wrong end of the day so I would have to come back.

The owner took us for a drink and a bite to eat and we quizzed him on why he was selling a viable business. He went on to explain that she was indeed a good fishing boat but he had had enough of the business. This did not seem right, and with a little more pressing, he gave away more. The skipper had been with him a long time and had done well, but he had been caught by his now wife, as so many had.

"Caught?" we asked

"The good fishermen earn very good money and the area here is quite poor," he said. "The young women here see the better fishermen as a target, they go out with the girls and have too much to drink and get them pregnant. The girl's father goes and makes the fishermen an offer that is not refused. It has been going on for years."

"I am still not with it?" asked Dad.

"He then has a young family and needs or wants more money. In my case my skipper was doing well but wanted more. He started landing in two places, one for him and one for me. An odd box I would have swallowed, but it got more. So he will not have a job at all now." You could see the sadness in the way he said it, that he did not enjoy what he had to do and was indeed doing.

We were soon back on the road to the airport, eventually clearing duty-free after buying a very nice cardigan for Heather and two woolly hats for the girls. The fun started again as we took off. The back of the plane was loaded with we thought were builders coming back to London to work. They were all the worse for drink and started singing just after take-off. Thankfully there was not any trouble and it was more like a firm's outing to the seaside.

When we got through the airport and returned to my car it had started to rain and it was dark. Driving around the M25 I kept being blinded by a flash of light. It was the headlights of cars being reflected of the top of a bald head in the back seat. I pointed out to Les would he mind moving or putting a hat on. He was very offended and moaned about it all the way home.

By the time we got home we had had so much fun and had laughed so much my jaw hurt. Only after getting home did learn about what had gone on in Ireland that day, and it bought us back to reality.

I did go back with Tim and have a ride but I had already bought her in my mind. A decision I have not regretted, although she has given me some heartache at times.

It was not until a few years later we found that, despite our checks, she had a paperwork problem. The authorities claimed she had a long-term stability problem. We spent a great deal of money putting this right, only to be pulled up time and again with the same argument, the paperwork must have been false or there must have been some incompetence. I am not sure which, but we did find that there was another boat of the same name and papers in our file. She was a different shape and design so our figures would not marry up. It got so bad we were detained in Ipswich. We had to pay a fine to have the boat released.

I did this after taking legal advice and went to sea. On my return I was contacted by the harbour master of Ipswich who luckily for me had no love for the MSA and other officials. He warned me there was a reception committee waiting for me and I was to keep calm. He would be there to help me and I was not to lose my temper. Oh that was hard! I argued that they had accepted my money so a contract had been agreed. This clearly stated that a sum of x-amount would be paid and the vessel would be released. There was no mention of anything else. They continued to argue the point until the harbour master stepped in.

He grabbed my arm and said: "Paul, I think we need to go for a walk." And off around the quay we went. I am and always will be grateful to him that day for saving a very difficult situation.

I knew some legislation was coming through and when challenged again, I just said: "I will cut the bow off then and shorten her."

"You can not do that," they replied.

"Watch me," I said.

In the end ,we cut of the front of the boat to bring her under the 15 metres limit: a waste of time and money especially as they had made a mistake but were not big enough to say so. What made it even worse, the surveyor who checked that we had indeed reduced the size of the vessel, then apologised for the aggravation he had caused.

Storm in the Wash

As a family we have worked in the Wash on numerous occasions. In the early days I was just the crew with my uncle Lol but several times, we (that is my generation) were on our own and would go there to catch that most prized of fish, whitebait, and more recently shrimp. The Gilson family first went to Boston, Lincolnshire on the Witham River to catch sprats; there is a long history of Essex boats going to Boston to catch sprats in the winter and skate in the summer so it was not a totally new experience. When they went there in the late 1960s they found that the sprats were small but the whitebait an ideal size.

I must admit my first impressions of Boston left me feeling rather under-whelmed; the harbour was once a very busy place but now is in full decay. The Pilgrim Fathers left here for the Americas and to be honest the quay side looked as though they had just left. It was a tip and when you considered the huge amount of fish landed there, it made no sense. Shrimp, cockles and mussels were the main catches by the local boats. Once a very big fishing fleet was based here with very large smacks working the North Sea but they had moved on long ago. I recall as young man seeing some of the smaller smacks working for pink shrimp or prawns as the locals called them, with a single beam trawl. These vessels were about 55ft long and only had a capstan to pull the gear up as they had done for probably a hundred years. It was no different than the fleet that had worked the area in the 1800s with the single beam trawl.

When we were first there, the port was still doing a reasonable trade with the near continent but it was what you can describe as a used-to-be kind of place. When I was last there in 2009, it was full of Polish workers employed on the land, and we realised while getting our supper that night, that we were were the only English speakers in what was a very packed fish and chip shop. This year we were up there looking for whitebait, and as I remember we had not done that well but stuck at it as there was not much going on locally. We had driven up from Southend in the early hours and got there just before high tide. We parked up to find that most of the locals were already at sea so after filling our water bottles we were off. We were here in the *Ros Beara* and the *Paul Peter*. Cousin Steve was with me while Eric Thomas and his crew Bob Whaller were aboard the *Paul Peter*. We proceeded down the river towards the sea, passing a couple of boats, coming home already cooking their catch of brown shrimp. Many of these boats were floating wrecks, but they worked. The boat that we moored alongside always made me smile as you could see the engine from the deck. It was past the red rust stage and was developing into a blob of iron oxide. As we passed another boat we knew, the owners waved and asked if we had heard the weather forecast. No, we indicated. "Breeze coming," was we got back from them. We gave them the thumbs up and carried on. As we carried on down river, it was bright and really quite pleasant with barely a breath of wind. With the ebb we had picked up speed and were soon clear of the river end and in the Freeman Channel. We were just passing one of our mates who was dredging for mussels when he called us on the VHF.

"Where do you think you're going?" he asked.

"Out to the Well," we answered.

"Be careful, youngsters, they are giving a ten north easterly forecast."

Now here was a conundrum! This was Ken Bagly (who we called the chairman, as he would have a comment ready at all times and encourage others to speak up while standing at the back of the room). He was frightened of nothing, and for whom I and many others had the greatest respect. He was telling us to be careful. But we were not going far. We would be okay.

"Thanks Ken, we will keep an eye out," I replied as we carried on out.

We deepened the water into the upper part of the Well and could see the light float (a cheap type of automatic lightship which looks like a great big pencil with a rubber stuck on the end). As the light was not rolling or bobbing about, we carried on. We started looking for fish going backward and forward across the deep water but after about half an hour we had seen nothing. As the tide was still with us we were going further to sea and we were soon past the float and heading northeast. When we had pasted the Knock buoy, we started to feel the gentle movement of a north east swell in the water.

This was a warning that we should have heeded. Eric, the skipper of the *Paul Peter*, commented that the clouds were moving very fast now. Our reply was that we were not in the sky. A very typical Gilson remark. However it was starting to freshen. We had not seen any fish marks at all, there was nothing that was worth a second look. It may well be that they had better knowledge than us and had run for shelter. It was coming to the point that we had to make a decision - keep going or turn round. The wind had picked up but I was mindful that we had not had a week's work for some time. "Let's go a bit further," I said to Eric.

We carried on for twenty minutes or so. Waves were starting to form on the swells and water was being blown across the tops of those waves. It was getting worse by the minute. We turned round, the waves were increasing in size all the time and within a half an hour we had started to surf.

The *Paul Peter* was soon looking very small as she was being picked up and pushed forward along ever-growing waves. Oh for a camera that afternoon, on one wave she went past us as though we had stopped, her speed probably well over ten knots. Likewise she was starting to disappear in the troughs. These were very big waves. We were also surfing, running down the leading edge of the waves. This was good fun to start with, the speed and the adrenalin flowing in buckets. I was soon to realise that we were nearly out of control as we plunged down, almost into the back of the next wave. The weight that was coming on the rudder was incredible when we were in dive mode and again as we slipped down the reverse side. We were rapidly getting into a survival situation. It was not fun any more; just pure hard work. Steve was acting as lookout as the waves came from behind, warning me of the bigger waves as they chased us along. He gave me half a cup of tea saying: "That's all you are going to get for some time, the milk bottle has fallen over and I cannot keep the kettle on the stove. To be honest we nearly lost the stove just now."

I realised for Steve to be showing some concern it was serious.

"You okay, Eric?"

"It's like being on a roller coaster," he laughed. But he was starting to drop back some distance behind us.

"I am going to tell the Coastguards we out here just in case," I said.

Over the VHF, I gave our location and destination and gave an estimated time of arrival. I would check in every half an hour, it was getting that bad. My arms were beginning to ache fighting the helm trying to keep her straight. The visibility was dropping now, reduced due to the spume being lifted off the water, great lines of spray floating about in the air. It really was not fun any more. The conversation between us had stopped; a sure sign that we were up against it. I have noted over the years that when people get scared they act in two ways, they either talk constantly or shut up. We were doing the latter. I had lost sight of the other boat and asked if they were okay

"It's a bit splashy outside but we are doing okay," Eric replied. Nothing scared Eric. He would often tell the tale of his few weeks of national service when he had the helm of a minesweeper crossing the Bay of Biscay in a force 10 and that all except he and another fisherman were seasick. He also had his faith. Ken's voice came over the radio asking our position.

"Just passing the Well inward bound," I replied.

"Tide's just flowing, we will be afloat soon," he explained.

"What's it like?"

"Flat calm; sun's out."

"Not like that here," he laughed.

"No it's not like that here either," I replied. "The only good thing is we are coming home like an express train."

"Keep in touch," Ken said.

It would be hard to say just how much wind there was, more than a gale, 9 to 10 possibly. Not that many people actually have been out or experienced that sort of wind speeds. I often get people tell me they were out in this and that but a proper storm, force 10 and above is rare.

A lifeboat in a storm force 10.

The written Beaufort Scale is the most accurate way of judging the weather visually: it was written a long time ago but it is spot on. On land, a 10 storm is seldom experienced but it can uproot trees and cause considerable damage.

At sea, it brings very high waves with long overhanging crests, the resulting foam is blown in great patches and forms dense white streaks along the direction of the wind. The surface of the sea takes on a white appearance, the tumbling movement of the sea becomes heavy and visibility is affected. We then had a new challenge as the wind would be on our side but at least the sandbanks would give us some shelter from the waves.

"Hold tight. Here we go." As we went round the buoy into the channel, she rolled nearly on her side and back: plates that had not moved in years took on a life of their own. Anything that could move did. I had braced myself with legs wide and gripping the wheel, tried to stand up straight. Waves were smashing into her side and walls of water were dropping on her deck. We were awash. Fortunately the sandbanks were starting to take the wave size down but the wind still managed to smash the waves into her side and cover us with spray. I could not see a thing, water was everywhere, washing around my feet, even in the wheelhouse. The radar was being affected by the water so we could not rely on that to see where we were going and I had to open the front window. The wind was just aft of amidships so hopefully, I told myself, not that much would come in. I warned Eric of what was to come; he was still ten minutes from the channel. It was getting better but we still had driving spray. We were not rolling so much now and Steve said he would have a look below just to check.

"Well?" I asked when he came back up.

"The bilge water has been up her sides and anything that could move has, but it's okay," he said.

"Looks like the wheelhouse needs a pump out," he added, as he looked down at the water that continued to wash back and forth around my feet.

I reported in to the Coastguard and said I would keep in touch until the Paul Peter was safe as well. The sand banks were having a greater effect now and after a couple of course changes in the narrow channel it was all but calm, except for the very strong wind that continued to make her roll about. I called Eric who had just entered the Freeman Channel and was rolling heavily.

"Had to wedge the door closed, it was sliding open and shut all on its own," he commented.

I could see the mussel boats just about to enter the river up ahead. A real sense of relief was washing over us and conversation was again flowing. As we entered the river, the Coastguard called us asking our position.

"We have just entered the River Witham" I replied, "and the *Paul Peter* is in the Freeman Channel so he should be okay now," I said, feeling something else was coming up.

"*Ros Beara,* could you assist a small coaster in distress outside Kings Lynn?"

I looked at Steve and stuck my head out of the window, only to have it nearly blow off. Our body language said a thousand words.

"Sorry, I would be endangering my crew and my vessel. We are not big enough to deal with the weather out there," I messaged back. That was the first and only time I have refused to go to someone's aid.

"Fully understand. We are sending the Skegness Lifeboat," the message came back.

We looked on the chart to see how far he would have to come and what a difficult launch he would have and I had another look outside just to make sure. No, it was out of the question and with that we watched a wooden target marker on the river side get torn to pieces by the wind.

"Good decision," we said as one.

As we approached our berth the *Paul Peter* was entering the river so we were all safe and sound and Steve soon had some dinner on. As we sat in the cabin eating our dinner, the tide was flowing very fast and we could see the quay side passing the porthole as though we were in a lift.

The storm was over for us but not the rest of the coast. Wells-next-the-Sea received the worst of the storm. The seawall failed, flooding the local golf course, and the force was such that several fishing boats were dragged from their moorings and left on the greens. A coaster was lifted onto the quay and deposited like a discarded toy. As for the Skegness Lifeboat men, they were not needed, but they had one hell of a ride to remember.

Ostrich

THIS IS A story that is not water based, but it is so funny I feel compelled to tell it. I have enjoyed the country life since I shot my first duck at the tender age of 11 and over the years have had much fun wondering around our beautiful countryside with some friends a dog or two, a gun and shooting, with luck, something tasty to eat.

For many years I went shooting with the same gang of guns. We had all met on a shoot in Kent in the 1990s and become very good friends. Although a very diverse bunch, we got on so well and knew how to be silly. The original shoot that we had joined, however, closed down and we split up. We all joined a couple of shoots near to our original shoot, so still managed to go shooting together a couple of times a year. But we had always talked about having a shoot of our own, and then one day it happened.

One of our number, George, had taken early retirement and been offered a shoot near Canterbury where he would be the game keeper and in charge. "Would you like to join the syndicate?" he asked. "It would be the same old faces and a few new ones to make up the numbers."

"When do we start, and what do you want me to do?" I replied instantly.

This shoot was unique in so many ways. We had a summer house to use as the shoot lodge and it had a kitchen where one of the new faces excelled with large bacon and egg rolls. Coffee and tea was abundant as were tales of big bags of duck and pheasant. On one occasion we had to move every one out side as too many birds were being shot in the kitchen.

Every drive on a shoot has a name: dog leg, square wood, nine acre, home wood, the gully - and on this shoot, we had the wilderness. The wilderness was well named as that was just what it was, a wilderness of about 8 acres of trees and brambles and all but impenetrable for a gang of beaters.

It was extra woodland that to start with we did not use. It was left until late in the season, when the trees had dropped their leaves and the brambles had died back. It was a jungle, and very dark. In the days when maps and charts were first made it would probably have read: "Here be monsters."

We did give it a try once early on and it was a disaster - it was dark and so thick you could not see each other. The beaters could not see over the brambles and you could not walk in a straight line, let alone keep walking in a beating line to push birds forward. Even the dogs on occasions would get tangled up in this dense undergrowth. But when we did get it to work, the birds did fly well and gave us some challenging shots. Having seen the potential, George set about opening out some of the denser parts where possible, and after many hours of strimming, a few pathways were created.

One of the things we wanted to do was to encourage young people to join and carry on our sport, so they were welcomed. With dads and granddads among us we soon had a gang of early teens joining in. I am not so sure it was the sport they came for as they got a £10 tip for being a beater. Now one of those silly things that we had been doing for years on the last drive of the day, was for one of us would shout out "Hi Ho," as in the Snow White and the Seven Dwarfs film, and another gun would reply "Hi Ho".

We would also call if a bird was going forward in the denser parts of the wood or drives. If anyone saw a fox, he'd call that out, just in case someone had a bigger cartridge in his bag to sort him out. Thus the scene was set.

We had been having a good day and had shot more birds than we should have by the time of day. (You don't want to shoot all the birds on your land in one go. You want to shoot for the whole season, so you set a mental bag limit.) George therefore decided to do the wilderness to slow the day down and he would also see if his hard work had made any improvements. We would have expected only to shoot a few in the wilderness, and the birds would have to fly high or through the trees requiring a very quick shot. We could clearly see some woodcock, as that very shy and difficult bird liked these quiet places. As we walked up the back of the wood to line it out I could hear the youngsters moaning about how difficult this looked and more like a jungle, they were being teenagers. I smiled. I was a walking gun, meaning I walk with the beaters and shoot birds going back or out the sides of the drive. I had at that time three English Springer Spaniels, not the best controlled I must admit, but they were good at their job of flushing birds and then retrieving them, hopefully when I had shot them.

We started the drive on a toot from a horn and had not got far in when it became clear that it was still far too dense to keep a line. Pheasants were running back past us under the thick bramble. Because the dogs use their noses, they did not see them. The young boys were starting to walk behind each other taking the easiest route through the brambles. I tried to encourage them to walk and beat in a line, but ten pounds was not enough to persuade them to go through this thick cover. The dogs yelped and made a noise, this does not normally happen, when it does it is possibly a rabbit; as on the whole they are very quiet.

The young beaters were talking among themselves, and I could hear them saying that there could be wild animals living here, their imaginations were running wild. I could not resist the temptation to play a prank.

"Ostrich, forward!" I screamed.

One of the granddads quickly took up story. "Over there!" he shouted, pointing in the area my dogs were hunting. None of the teenagers could see because they were too short to see over the brambles. They could not see me or Granddad either.

"Did you see the size of that?" I asked Granddad.

"No" he replied. "But I did see what it did to the brambles as it ran through them."

This conversation was heard by the boys, who at first were silent. Then you could hear them start to talk but only in whispers.

"What was that all about?" one said.

I heard another reply: "There was a lot of noise in front of me but I could not see anything."

His neighbour just said: "An ostrich?"

The drive was not that good, a few birds were shot going forward but I did get a couple going back. As we walked to the next drive, George sidled up to me. "An ostrich?" he asked, wide-eyed and smiling.

"That's what it looked like to me. I only got a glimpse - it was very fast, ask the beater that was next in line, he saw something as well!"

"Something went through there, George, and it was big," Granddad replied.

George walked away with his dogs and was heard to say "An ostrich?" as he shook his head. This was all done just within ear shot of a couple of the youngsters as we walked down the ride. A legend was made; the other guns soon got the drift, with one commenting that it did not come his way, another saying he heard a lot of noise coming from the side and it must have crossed the road in to the wood opposite. It was sealed as we had a drink in the lodge after the shoot, when one of the locals said that an ostrich had escaped from the local wildlife park a couple of years back and had not been seen since.

A week passed before the team reassembled. We were attacking our now very large and delicious bacon and egg roll, and the youngsters were huddled together as though they were trying to hide, or make out that the grown-ups weren't there. Our cook looked at me as I handed the rolls around to the guns and guests and gave me a little wave of his head, beckoning me over to him. He spoke softly from behind his moustache, his lips barely moving: "The boys are talking ostrich," and then he winked.

Pegs were drawn and the day began with the usual banter and ribbing of each other. We'd shot a good few birds by lunch time and George had worked out the strategy for the afternoon and the wilderness was part of it. We again lined up at the back of the wood, we tried to keep the youngsters apart, otherwise they would tend to talk and not do their jobs properly.

As I walked past the first young beater, he asked: "Will we see the ostrich?"

"I don't know, but George has told me that the bird feeders here had been knocked down!" (The bird feeders were made from small plastic drums and filled with seed a hole was made in the bottom and the birds would peck the seeds from them.) They had fallen down because the ground was soft but I did not say that. Once we were all lined up, the horn blew and we set off.

We had not gone far when further along the line, someone shouted: "Ostrich, forward!"

"There it goes!" The guns were joining in. The atmosphere was electric, it was hard not to laugh out loud. The boys were in total confusion.

"I never saw anything," said one.

"That was Granddad," said another not believing that he could be telling lies. Granddad, however, was right up for it.

When we finished the drive, he was there nodding his head.

"Did you see it?" I asked.

"See it! It looked me in the eye. A big brute, with beady eyes frightened the life out of me. I only saw its head over the brambles. Has anyone a flask? A drop of gin will calm my nerves."

The boys were all hooked. There was an ostrich living in the wilderness! As we walked on there was muffled laughter among some of the guns.

Looked at me over the brambles!" one repeated, laughing.

Now on shoot days, we would often have a guest or two amongst us, and today was no different. They were as confused as the boys and the guests were trying to understand what on earth was going on. After the last drive of the day, we walked back to the vehicles and one of our guests asked George what was going on. "Don't ask, it would take too long to explain," he replied.

Our poor guests had not a clue, what they were thinking goodness knows, that we were all mad, I suppose. I felt we needed to take our joke a bit further and sought the help of a friend of mine who runs an antique business. I arrived at the shoot the following week early with a large box. I explained to George what I wanted him to do and he took the box. As the guns and beaters arrived, the usual banter was dotted with mentions of the ostrich. George came in with the box after checking out the first drive of the day making sure there were birds in it. He gave me the box to open- out came an ostrich egg.

"The keeper next door found this last year and he heard about what we had seen," George said in a voice, just loud enough for several of the young beaters to hear. The look on their young faces was priceless, they were all totally hooked.

"Are we doing the wilderness today?" one asked.

"Probably the last drive of the day," George replied.

The air was thick with excitement. That last drive could not be coming fast enough. Our chef gave me another bacon and egg roll.

"Gilson, you are unreal," he said whispering through his moustache. "When are you going to tell them?"

"Not yet," I replied, "not yet".

Little did I know that Granddad had something up his sleeve, literally. We had had a good day, so we were all relaxed and assembled at the start of the wilderness drive. The beaters were talking in very hushed tones, not wanting to get told off for scaring the birds, but enough to make a low mumble and earn a swift look from some of the guns, telling them to be quiet. We set off as the horn was sounded and once we had got in the thickest area there was a shout. It was Granddad.

"Get down!"

"There it goes!" said his grandson.

"Are you all right? It ran right over you!"

"It ran over my back!"

"I know, I saw it, there is a foot print on your back!"

"Quick get up if you are okay we don't want to get left behind."

When the drive finished, the grandson was ecstatic. He was telling his mates about the ostrich that knocked him down and then ran over him.
He had definitely been on the floor. The front of his coat with caked in mud, and sure enough on his back was a three-toed foot print. Brilliant, I thought, Granddad must have had something to do with this. As we walked back, even some of the guns were now believing that we had an ostrich in the wood, because I had been several paces away from the action. The young beaters were examining the coat and asking all the questions.

"Was it heavy? Did you see it? Did it hurt?"

Grandson was full of it, his chest puffed out. "George, an ostrich ran over me!"

"Did you see it, Paul?" George asked, giving me a very quizzical look. I shrugged my shoulders. As we walked back there were many confused people about, me being one of them. Our chef walked with me back to the vehicles.

"Okay, how did you do that?"

"I have got to say I had nothing to do with it, I am as surprised as you."

Grandson wore his coat like a badge of honour virtually everyone had a look at the foot print.

I sought out Granddad, as the boys were all in a gang in front and very excited. I hoped we could have a quick word. Granddad had other ideas.

"I will talk you through it later, let them enjoy the moment," he said with a grin that would match that of Cherie Blair.

Back in the lodge we were having our post-shoot debate; but there was only one topic of conversation. The boys were all outside. "Come on Granddad what happened?" I asked.

He looked round to make sure no one could see and produced a wooden frame from his pocket shaped like an ostrich foot.

"I knocked him to the ground then hit him in the back with the foot," he replied, so casually.

I looked forward to the next Saturday when it would all start again, but unfortunately Granddad had to own up because things were getting out of hand. People had started to talking to the papers and getting television involved.

Oh well, some legends don't stand up for too long, but this one was so very good while it lasted.

Sprats Galore

O NE OF MY favourite types of fishing is sprat fishing. In years gone by this was possibly the mainstay of the Thames fisheries but like most things in recent years it has declined. Not because of a shortage of fish, but just a change in eating habits. Sprat and herring were a staple part of the local diet, either fresh, smoked, pickled or in the case of sprats, tinned and then called sild or brisling. I believe its downfall was the fact that it smells when cooking. The modern housewife does not want a smelly kitchen or house.

We use a net called a Larsen Trawl, but over the years it has changed from being square to a large rectangle. In local history, the method used was Stow-boating or Stow-boarding. This consisted of a net that was attached to two large bulks of timber. These act as the mouth that held the net open, which in turn was attached to the anchor cable. The net was tapered, as it is now, and looked like a sock or stocking, and a very long one at that. The smack or bawley would sail or motor around in the tide way looking for a show of birds, gulls picking sprat from the water, or go to a popular spot. (The Chapman buoy or light house were the local favourites.) It would drop anchor, pay the net away and wait for the fish to be washed into the net by the tide. Basic as it may seem, it worked very well and many good catches were taken; the method survived through to the 1960s when the *Saxonia* owned by Young's was still stow-boating for whitebait. It was such a prized catch that a skiff would take the fish ashore to Canvey Island, where a van would be waiting to take it to top London restaurants. Sprats and whitebait have a very limited shelf life, so with no sensible cooling or refrigeration the sooner it got to the customer the better. Sprats normally arrive about the third week in November, the guide date being the Lord Mayor's Show in the City of London. Sprats would be landed in Leigh or the former Southend Corporation Loading Pier.

This particular year, we were landing in Leigh at Bell Wharf. We had developed a good team, with two carrying boats and a tow boat. We found that half of the best fishing time we were spending hauling. This gave us the idea of bringing another carrying boat. I would shoot with one boat and catch say 8 to 10 tons, then as soon as the wings of the net were passed over, we'd part up and go and shoot with the other boat that had been watching the shoal. By the time we hauled again the other boat hopefully was ready to shoot again. The *Ina K* was that other boat run by Dad's friend Colin Knapp, with his son Ken and his old school chum Nate as crew. On the *Anja* there was Dad and Andy, leaving me on the *Marco Polo* with Tim whom I would only see at the beginning and end of the day. We had invested in the new colour sounders for fish finding and they were brilliant once we had got used to them. We had been fishing for several weeks and we had developed a good routine. The fishing had been a bit scratchy to start, but was improving every day as more fish entered the river. We had landed in Leigh on the last trip. Colin and I had laid at Bell Wharf - the first place you can land when you come into Leigh. Dad landed in the middle of the town at Timber Wharf (also known as Theobald's Wharf, but renamed by locals because timber was shipped here up to the 1990s).

We had been hoping to get an order for boxed sprats, but until we could prove that there was enough fish to support a targeted fishery and the sample was good, the canning factory was reluctant to start us on. They needed a count of 75 to 90 fish per kilo. We were therefore not going flat out as although we enjoyed the job, we did not like catching fish for fish meal. Fish meal is used as fertiliser, animal feed and some times fish food. Sprats are very oily and we were told that some was used in making margarine, as a fact I am not sure but that was our belief. The price difference must also come into it boxed was £75 a ton and meal was £45 but we had to pay the transport. This particular day we had made a turnout time of 1 am at high tide. We assembled at the wharf and Dad and Andy walked up the high street to Timber Wharf. Colin and I got aboard and set about starting up and getting underway. As we had time, we washed the wharf off and cleaned it ready for our catch later in the day. As I told Tim to let go, Dad's voice came over the radio.

"My sounder's on the blink or the creek is full of fish. I cannot see a bottom. The screen is solid red."

Tim heard this on deck and laughed. "Dad's been playing with the buttons again," he chuckled.

"We have just pushed her of the quay and it is solid. The middle of the creek is full. I have 6 feet of fish under the boat," Dad said. He was very excited and shouted from the wheelhouse window: "Unbelievable!"

Colin followed him down the creek with me behind. I had the deepest draught so I had to be very careful. Dad's draught was 5 feet, Colin's just over 6 feet, and mine, well about 7 feet 6 inches. They turned their lights out so as not to blind me and we moved slowly out and down the creek. I was, to say the least, concerned. I could not see the bottom and going aground was not an option I wished to consider. I would expect some propeller wash but I should still see the bottom. Colin came on the radio to Dad.

"It is not your set, Pete. Mine is saying the same."

I tried to drop back and let them get clear. Not only did I have the disturbance of two boats, but we had a shoal of fish here as well. Oh, I could see it now The *Polo* stuck on the side of the creek as daylight revealed her to the dog walkers and commuters going up to London on the train. As Dad was so much further down the creek, he put on a small light on his afterdeck. The result was snow or a glut of seagulls picking sprats out of the water. Dad and Colin were chatting and comparing notes on what they could see. They were already in deeper water in the bay, while I still had to go round the first bend. The creek was full of birds and the water was full of fish. I started to turn at the first buoy and she was starting to go and then she touched. She leaned over and slid down the other side. I had just caught the corner and that was the easy corner.

Tim was on the bow trying to keep me in the creek. "Over there ten degrees. Straight round you go, the buoy is there," he pointed. We made our way towards the Ray. The Ray is a deep water channel that runs from Benfleet down towards Southend Pier, the lower half has water for our size boats at all times of the tide so when Dad entered the Ray he would have 25 to 30 ft of water under the boat. Oh, Dad and Colin were getting so excited, the fish were top to bottom and they still had not even got to the Ray. I was taking my time. Dad said he would push on and get out of the Ray and see what there was outside so we could start work straight away. Tim put on his oil skins, expecting to start work immediately. We could not shoot the gear in the Ray as there is always too much debris in it from anchors to old moorings and general rubbish that all and sundry have dumped there over the years. Dad came on the radio: "You will never believe it, the Ray is empty. I will push on down to the pier."

Colin was shearing about looking for fish as he got into the Ray. He too said nothing there and shaped up the Ray as Dad went down. I was still carrying fish in the creek and if we were anywhere other than here I would want to shoot into the tide and up the creek.

Incredibly, I was practically outside my own house, which is on the banks of the Estuary, and my wife was sleeping only 250 yards away. I carried on down the creek and headed for my mooring. Dad was rushing about as if demented going this way and that looking for fish. He had had a big adrenaline rush. Colin was nearly as bad going over the Ray bank to the deeper water. I could not do that with my draught. Colin was soon over the bank and he too could see nothing. Dad was down to the pier and he was saying he had a blue screen. I deepened the water into the Ray and from solid fish there was nothing. The fish were right in the shallows. I turned up the Ray and slowly went up towards Benfleet. After about half a mile, I started to see some fish. It was just a few - the main shoal was in the creek. I turned and went back down towards my mooring, and as I passed the end of the creek, I turned as if I was going back into Leigh. Sure enough they were still there. I told the others what I could see, and apart from the fish in the creek, they had seen nothing. We decided to wait on the mooring until daylight when the fish would have to be in the deep water. I picked up my mooring and the others came alongside. Tea was drunk and a decision was made to sleep for a couple of hours. As I have said before, I needed no encouragement to hit my bunk. Dad as usual said he would sit and watch what happened. After what seemed like five minutes, he was calling us, excitedly.

"I have watched fish go past us for two hours," he said. "It has only just eased off, they must be down to the pier by now and daylight is in the sky."

He had let Andy go and they were off out the Ray. Colin followed close behind, with myself as usual bringing up the rear. By the time we were out the Ray, daylight was with us and the Gut - the area of deeper water from the Ray to the Boom - was full of birds. All kinds of birds looking or feeding on sprats. The amount of fish was just amazing. The screen was showing red with hint of brown. This was a serious amount of fish, brown is the darkest colour meaning the fish are very dense. The excitement was becoming infectious. "Come on Paul, I am shooting. Just come and get the ends!"

I pushed her on and quickly was alongside. "What do you reckon?" he asked, meaning how long do you think we need to tow for?

"Five minutes, top whack," I said confidently, as ropes were released and wires attached. We moved apart.

"Three aft," he said, meaning 30 feet of wire on the stern. We give the bottom wire 6 feet more so the net opens wide enough to allow the fish in. It has a sinker on it, a large weight weighing some 200lbs. My winch was in the wheelhouse with me. Dad's winch was on deck and Andy operated it. Tim was aft watching the marks.

"Right ho!" he said and came into the wheelhouse to look at what we had shot on. "Corr that's all right," he chortled. That was an understatement.

"Solid red," I told Dad.

"No, brown."

"Digitising," I said, referring to when the sounder is fooled by the thickness of the fish. The fish is so dense the signal bounces of the top of the shoal and the digital read out actual reads the top of the shoal and not the sea bed, this does not happen often.

"Me too," Dad replied.

"One minute," I said.

"Two minutes," said Andy and Tim, who were watching the gear.

"She is starting to boil." Tim said.

Andy was pointing at the gear and said something to Dad.

"We are slowing, Dad, I think we better do it," I told him.

We bumped back alongside and started to haul. Colin spoke to say he felt there was even more in front of us.

"Line them up. I will be straight with you," I replied.

As we stopped the boats moving the net came to the top. The gulls were straight at her diving and picking fish up from the water. It was a good haul but she was not full up enough according to Dad .

"Way you go there, not tight and they're all alive."

The ropes were let go and I was off to find Colin who was only 100 yards away. I was straight alongside and the fish was in the brown as we started to shoot. I connected up and we split up. I had to be careful as I was now very close to the end of Southend Pier. We put the brakes on and we were fishing again.

"Solid brown, sounding on the top, four metres brown, "Colin said. "Brown top to bottom."

"Same here," I replied. The speed was dropping and Ken was looking aft with his thumb up. It was hard for me to see but the speed had dropped to nothing. "That's enough Colin, I would prefer two hauls than one."

"Let's make sure." he said.

Dad came on: "Eight ton, nice and easy. They were not crammed in."

The tow was getting longer.

"That's enough Colin, loosing my steering".

"Let's do it then." he replied.

"I will come to you other wise I will catch the pier."

Alongside and heading south away from the pier, as the wires came up, a whale appeared behind us. The net was near to full. Colin will be happy, I thought. We soon had it going round his net drum. Fish were spilling out as many had only just gone in. I did not leave him this time, as he would need turning round when the sleeve comes alongside. By the time we had got to the smaller meshes, the net was getting wider, thankfully they were all alive. Colin waved and I put the *Polo* in gear and turned the pair round.

The idea is that the sleeve with the fish in runs alongside the boat aft to forward. The bag is then hauled out level with the hold and swings in to be emptied into the fish room. The bag when full lifts a ton a time, and getting bumped by it is not a good idea. All the sections were full, but fortunately all was alive. The first bag was soon aboard and I was sent off to fish again with Dad. As before, he had lined the fish up and we shot in a similar place to last time, the haul was only another three minutes and it looked good. I did the same for Dad, this time turning the *Anja* round so we could pick up the sleeve amidships. We put aboard two lifts before Dad sent me off. Colin was down in the water, possibly half full, I thought. We shot again and it was still a very good mark. Brown top to bottom. Four minutes this time and we were still just off the pier head. The same routine. After another couple of bags I left him. Dad was just finishing. He was full down below and had several bags on deck. "How many?" I asked

"About sixteen," Dad replied. "I don't mind a few more as it is so calm and we have not far to go."

Fish were still running down toward us, although it was nearly low water. Again we were only just off the pier, the rest of the fleet of sprat boats were about and we could hear them talking on the VHF They were several miles to the east of us and had found nothing but there were coming our way as they had been listening to us talking. I was back alongside Dad and the net was going over again. We took our time as we had got our day's work, we just needed to top it up. Within minutes we were passing the pier again. Tim asked if I wanted some tea as things had been a bit hectic.

"Is the Pope a Catholic?"

"Don't know about that sort of stuff," he replied. "If you don't get time now, you might not get one until after we have hauled."

The reading was good but only red and the tide had stopped moving so we would not get the yield that we had earlier. It was still a good reading so we gave this haul a full five minutes. I drank my tea while we hauled. The gear was on the surface and it looked better than the first one. I looked over to Colin and he was still hauling. The *Ina* was down to deck level. We turned the gear round and got it alongside and the first bag was soon aboard, it was better than the first one. After the hold was full, the decks were pounded off on both boats, the *Anja* carried 13 tons down below and 8 to 9 tons on deck as a rule. The *Ina* carried 24 below and 10 on deck. She was like a submarine with more boat under than above the water, for that was how Colin liked it. When we started to load on deck, it took more time as the fish had to be spread evenly to keep the boat stable. It became very difficult to move about as you may well be walking in two feet of fish. We put five tons on Dad and he sent me off to Colin, as he continued getting his fish aboard. Colin had only just finished he had six or more tons on deck. I went alongside and asked him what he wanted to do.

"I think we can put a few more bags on deck," he replied.

I knew what he would say but I did have to ask. He let the gear go and prepared to shoot again. We did not have to go far back to the face of the pier. Looking over to Dad, I could see the fish above the rails. The *Anja* looked sick and he was still putting fish aboard. We shot again with Colin, and I asked him how many more he was going to want. I knew it was wrong to ask. I saw him smile at me from his wheelhouse window. He had twice 10 tons, he said. Oh well, we were on a good reading but with no tide at all we may have to tow for as long as ten minutes. I asked again: "How many more?"

"A few more, let's make sure."

We had now passed the pier. We had not fished this bit before and the sounder went brown again. The fish had dropped to the bottom and there was a hell of a lot of it. "I think that will do, Colin."

"Give it another minute" he replied. I was getting a bad feeling. This was going to yield very well as the fish was now on the bottom and the depth we were fishing meant we would be fishing at our best.

"She is slowing again."

The crew of the Ina K loading sprats. With her fish room already full, they are loading the deck. Colin Knapp is on the port side, next to the wheelhouse.

She was full, once we had it alongside and it was obvious that we had enough. It was a struggle to keep the fish moving they had started to die. We had our work cut out Nate and Ken were pulling the fish into the bag and then trimming the fish on deck. We were soon above the rail with fish and we still had several tons to put on deck. "Shall I let these go?" I asked.

"No, we can get a few more on."

The boys kept pushing fish about and another bag was opened and pushed about. They were starting to slip off, they were stacked so high. It was becoming a job to empty the bag as we could not get it high enough for the fish to come out of the bag when it was opened. They were piled high behind the whale back, the water was six inches deep on deck and fish were swimming out the scuppers and back again. "How many more?" Colin asked.

"Two bags but they will be big ones."

"Make it two small ones, then a big one and we keep that one on deck hanging from the derrick."

As the last bag came aboard there was a bump, and the boat slewed round. We were aground the tide was coming in and we were being carried back into Leigh. Dad jogged over to speak to us.

"I think that will do, I have run out of boat to put them on"

The *Anja* was loaded to the gunwales, any more would be stupid.

We put the *Polo* back on the mooring and had a much earned and needed cup of tea and a sandwich, waiting for water back in to Leigh. Stories abounded about who had done what and never having done this before. I ordered two trucks that should be okay. I thought sixty tons capacity would be enough as it should only be fifty tons but there would be water and the more that went on the one truck the more we would be paid. I know it was wrong but we were only bending the rules. We landed in Leigh two hours later, the crane or Neal as we called her, was soon at work grabbing the fish from the deck and then the hold. The *Anja* was first as she was drawing less water than the *Ina*.

The truck driver came over and voiced his concern over the amount we had and how much was already on his lorry. He felt that he would have his load just from the *Anja*. He knew that the *Ina* carried much more, another truck was ordered. He left as Colin came alongside and the second truck was lined up. To be honest it was a sight - the *Ina* was a floating fish box. There was a bit of boat visible at the front and another bit at the back - the rest was fish. I dread to think what passers by must have thought.

When the deck was clear, the driver felt he was over half full and it was not long before he said that, although he did not mind some over the top, his truck was not big enough to take any more. He did remind us of a trip the previous year, when he had a very wet load of fish on and each time he braked and fish shot over the front of the cab. So loading the third lorry was started. We were all down the *Ina*'s hold, shovelling the last nine tons to the middle to be grabbed out. The energy levels were starting to droop. When the last grab went out we were all out of puff and just lent on our shovels and laughed.

Next day we found out that the *Anja* landed 28 tons, the *Ina* K 37 tons - an incredible total of 65 tons. We never had a day like that again.

Nowadays, I would not know what to do with any amount of sprats. The factories have all gone and the factory ships sold or broken up. The fish meal plant is still there and has taken fish recently from Leigh, but I do think it is wrong to send such good fish for meal when we could eat it. We worked out that our total fishing time was under half an hour, hard work but great fun. We landed over 200 tons for the week.

My happiest memories of Colin Knapp and Dad, are of their smiling faces that day and Dad saying that he had run out of boat.

I dedicate this story to those of us still alive,
as we were privileged to have taken part in that day's work.
For Ken, Tim and Andy, lest we never forget these great days!

The Snake

EARLY ONE MORNING we were getting under way from our quay at Barling. It was early April, a flat calm but with a mist so thick you could not see the seawall. Daylight would be coming soon but at this time, it was very dark as there was no moon, and I would have to be careful going down the creek.

We had cast off and thrown the ropes back onto the quay. I had turned the lights off to give myself better vision. There was a scream from the after deck and my crew came rushing in to the wheelhouse.

"Snake, snake" he was shouting.

He was scared stiff: "There is a snake on the after-deck, it's huge," he was sobbing. "Oh, I was so lucky." Tears were running down his face.

"Are you sure?" I asked puzzled.

"It's coiled up and its tail is lying across the net."

"Go and have another look."

"Please," he sobbed. "Don't make me go out there it is huge."

I could not make this out. Why would a snake of such a huge size be lying on a cold deck at this time of day? It just did not add up.

"Go and have another look, I cannot leave the wheel yet nor put the lights on as we will get ashore on one side or other with the tide so high so I must watch what I am doing."

"Oh God, please don't make me"

"Go and have a look."

He went outside but was quickly back, sobbing and tears flowing down his cheeks. There was enough water to irrigate a desert. It was embarrassing, a young man falling to bits over a snake he said was so huge he was frightened for his life on the back of a fishing boat! I had not been up long and I was starting to ask myself: was this a dream?

He was now crouched in the corner of the galley sobbing and hiding his face begging me to get rid of it. I tried to calm him down but he would have none of it.

In a couple of minutes, I would be clear enough to stop the boat and check. My mind was working overtime: snakes do not like the cold, why would it be so exposed? It should be hiding, I told myself.

We entered the Violet, a deeper and wider creek, and I stopped the boat and turned on the lights. I walk aft not knowing what I was going to meet; I could not believe my eyes.

"Quick," I called out, "come and see this"

"No, no, get rid of it," he screamed.

"I can promise you it will do you no harm."

"I know you, it's just a trick," he shouted back between sobs.

"I will come with you."

"And you won't turn the lights off?"

"No, I will be with you."

He came out of the wheelhouse and made his was along the deck nearly too where I was standing. He still could not see clearly.

"Is it still there?" he asked.

"Yes it's still there," I replied. "I can assure you it will do you no harm."

He came that bit further just so he could see the deck and the snake and was greeted by an old straw hat or boater that had come unravelled leaving a long tail running across the deck. I just shook my head, what was I to say, what could I say?

"It could have been a snake," he said defensively.

I returned to the wheelhouse and proceded to sea.

"A snake?" I kept saying to myself and out loud, "A snake!"

Paul, net mending.

Net Mending on a Cold Night

A s I HAVE said before, I got on very well with Colin Knapp and his son Ken. They had been having trouble mending a big pair trawl net that they had torn and had mentioned this to Dad. They were mending it at home next to his garage. Dad suggested I should pop in on my way home from the yard and see if I could help. We were home because it was blowing north-easterly and it was very cold thanks to snow showers.

I arrived at Colin's about 1 pm and my help was gratefully received. Colin and Ken were very good with paint brushes, carpentry and even mechanics but were not so good at mending. I make no excuses. I was, and still am, useless at the above but I can mend. It must be a different mind-set because as long as I have some clues and some net to work with I can put it back together, for much cheaper than buying new gear. The trouble was their net was old -it was second-hand when they got it - so there were many different mesh sizes and it had been repaired many times before. This was not all bad because it was giving me some reference points.

We got stuck in, pulling the trawl one way and then the other, mending sometimes several directions at once, pulling all the loose ends together. Time soon passed as the stories flowed between us. Some soup and bread turned up from the kitchen and lights were turned on as darkness fell. It was getting very cold when Colin nudged me.

"Here, get some of this down your neck." He passed me a tumbler with some spirit in and I promptly gulped it down. Sure enough it gave me a nice warm feeling and we carried on mending.

We came to a bit where we had no clues. A large piece was missing from the side where the shape of the net is made. We had to try several different cuts to get it to the right shape. This part of the net is called the salvage and is normally made from three meshes from each panel. It gives strength and protects the shape or cut so when the net gets torn you can open the salvage to make a clear mend.

This had all gone, so we made many false starts to get this right, but it was coming together. What also kept coming were more glasses of this warming spirit. I can still feel its warmth as it ran down my throat. Our stories were getting more bizarre and we were laughing and giggling a lot. What the neighbours were thinking, goodness knows. But the cold was forgotten as we stitched away. More glasses of the nectar were shared round and I was getting a bit of a warm glow around my cheeks and the net was starting to take shape.

Colin suggested that we stopped work as time was getting on and there was quite a bit of snow on the ground.

"We're okay," Ken and I replied.

"It's ten o'clock"

"Oh shit, I will be in for it when I get home," I blurted out. We quickly pulled the net into the garage and I said my good byes.

When I got home Heather was actually quite calm about the whole thing but dinner was not quite what it would have been when it was prepared several hours earlier.

"Have you been drinking?" she asked.

"Colin gave us a glass of whisky to keep us going and keep us warm, why?"

"Oh nothing," was her reply.

I thought I had got away with it, but obviously not. The next day, I went round to Colin's to see how we had done to find that we had nearly finished the net but had also nearly finished a bottle of his best Scotch whisky. I had not drunk it before, but I have done since.

Happy Days!

Dunkirk Spirit

Part Two

ONCE MOORED UP in Dunkirk, we were looking forward to our hotel and a wash. The thought of a hot shower was spurring us on after a long day; the sun and wind burn now taking its toll on our faces. We carried our very heavy bags across the other boats and stood on the quay side, with Peter again reading the instructions and the directions to get to Best Hotel. "A blue elephant?" he said, bemused.

Little did we know then, we would spend several hours searching for this blue elephant, but not understanding why. It was like a scene from Last of the Summer Wine: a bunch of middle aged men lost in France needing somewhere to rest, but looking for a blue elephant! After a bus ride and much cursing, we managed then to get off at the wrong stop. We walked on several miles along the road, and in the distance could see some buildings, but not our hotel. Further on we pressed, in silence and exhausted. I could see what looked like another hotel and then, like a mirage, I saw the trunk of a blue elephant! To say we were relieved was an understatement; the blue elephant was the logo of a chain of car-wash businesses. We established that there were indeed three hotels on the site. Ours was basic, but not as bad as the one next door, which appeared to be made from old containers and welded together and covered in Artex. We checked in without too much stress and we were by this time all knackered. Peter and Cameron tried to explain that the directions were not as good as they could be, but they should not have wasted their time, as we had a young Basil Fawlty running the place. The hotel telephone kept ringing. He answered and passed the telephone to Cameron. "For me?" Cameron said in disbelief. The young Basil nodded and gave him the phone.

*Endeavour's motley crew, with Josh, our RN rating just after he
had put us alongside in the lock at Dunkirk.*

Cameron taking the initiative said: "Bonjour! Ah okay.. well, err…. we have just…yes, very poor. Look for the blue elephant. Yes we know…"

Once in our room, we put the television on BBC news and there we were being described by the presenter. "In the middle of the lock, centre of the screen is a green boat called *Endeavour*." Peter got very excited.

The only good thing about our room was the shower. It was so strong we could have pressure-washed the barnacles of the bottom of the boat with it. After freshening up, we returned to the restaurant/bar. Graham and Trevor were already there, and Cameron and Fin came in just behind us. Several bottles of Leffe beer were already on the table and more were ordered. Oddly, the menu was in French and my colleagues seemed to forget that we were indeed in France. Cameron came to the rescue with his translation: egg, chips and steak, although the steak turned out to be a beef burger. Basil was hovering about and eventually we managed to get our dinner ordered. We tried in vain to get just egg and chips for Peter (he does not eat meat, poor thing) but you could only get egg, steak and chips. I played the white man and did a swap. The food filled a need, but we would not eat here again. Remarkably, we made our way through all the hotel's supply of Leffe that evening. This would not be the last time this would happen over the next few days. But Basil got very agitated and as 10 o'clock approached he ushered us out of the bar and closed up and went home, an early night ensued.

Next day, Peter and I were dressed up in blazers, collars and ties. We had to be at the town hall for a memorial service, then to the site of a massacre of British soldiers. Cameron managed to communicate with Basil that we would need a taxi to go back to the harbour as we were miles from nowhere; this would work out a very expensive necessity over the weekend. While we waited for our transport, a young woman came in followed by an older man who thanked Cameron profusely. They were the people he had helped with directions to the hotel on the phone the night before. Cameron asked what they were doing here.

"We work for Central TV," the woman replied.

Fin, our own media expert was there so fast I heard the protective cap come off the Exocet and the missile launch.

"Oh and what do you do?" he asked.

"I present the news clips, we are here to cover the celebrations."

"We may be able to help you there," said Fin, not slow in coming forward when a good looking woman was about. You could see the glazed look in what turned out to be the cameraman's eyes.

The Chumly, with John Hoskins at the helm and Miss "Cool" on board, about to re-enter the lock in Dunkirk.

Fin explained about our boat and why we were there. The reporter was not interested in what he had to say, but she played along. She needed someone from the central England, she told us, a little bored. Well, then Fin got very excited explaining how we could help there, because our new friend, John Hoskins, was from Leicester in his boat the *Cholmondesleigh*, or the *Chumly* to his friends.

"Oh cool," she replied. The cameraman even came to life. "Could you introduce us?"

Cameron replied: "He is a very nice bloke. I am sure it will not be a problem."

Oh great, cool," was her reply.

"Come on," said Graham. "The taxi is here." We waved our goodbyes and said in unison: "Oh, cool."

We travelled along the coast back to Dunkirk, one of two routes we would be taking over the next few days and ending up 35 Euros lighter in the pocket. It was another cold day and our Navy cadet Josh was there as well as the *Ferry Nymph*'s cadet Candy. They had been instructed to help us clean up and dress the boat. (To dress the boat you put up flags and bunting, the flags should not spell out a message.) We put up the few flags we had and had a wipe round. Josh and Candy were telling us that they felt they had the best time of all the cadets, they had been allowed to steer and not just make the tea on the trip over like the cadets on other boats.

Cleaning up did not take long. Cameron went off to help John and Graham and Trevor went sightseeing. We agreed to meet in a bar at the end of the harbour around midday after we had finished at the town hall. As Peter was talking to people on the quay, I went and did what I do best:

I drank tea with Jonathan on the *Ferry Nymph* and we exchanged what I would call very good banter. I have found that friends just appear. You cannot go looking, they just turn up, sometimes it takes years to develop, others five minutes. Jonathan and crew were the five minute-version nice guys, the lot of us just like big kids and long may it continue.

After winding the Nymph's crew up, I took a walk along the quay and looked back at *Endeavour*. She needs more bunting I thought. One of our trust members is a semi-retired farmer called Jeremy Squire. He has a very nice yacht called *April Rose* and he had followed the convoy over to Dunkirk and was now moored in the yacht marina. He had been to Dunkirk before and knew his way round, so I rang him and asked if he could tell me where I could find a chandlers to buy some bunting. No problem, he would check out the two that he knew of at the top of the quay above the marina. That left me wandering along the line of boats and thinking how unsuitable many of these boats were for the job they had been chosen for in 1940. That word "miracle" comes up time and again when you look around at what happened.

"Oi Gilly," Cameron called from *Chumley*, as he waved me over. I entered the plastic green house that John had created on *Chumley*; it gave him a warm and dry saloon yet was easily removed. He had all round vision and it had given him space to live aboard in. John is a very good raconteur and jokes and stories flowed from his lips. The most amazing was about his boat: he had shortened her name because no one could spell her proper name or even say it correctly "*Cholmondesleigh*." She had once belonged to the 1940s comedian Tommy Trinder, who had taken her to the Dunkirk beaches himself. With him on that trip was Bud Flanagan, best known now as the singer of the introductory song for the Dad's Army TV show: "Who Do You Think You Are Kidding Mr Hitler?" John had found that there was a small entry in Flanagan's biography, saying that he had only been to France once and that was only to the beach. True or not it, was a good story and I believed it.

Cameron had already given him the heads up on the reporter and to my surprise she had already been to see him. John said he would see us at the town hall in half an hour's time. As Peter and I walked slowly to the town square, we could tell the weather was getting very warm. We went for a coffee at one of the bars around the square and sat outside in front of the town hall, looking at the many statues of knights and grand folk on its façade, and a very big guy walking towards us.

"Hallo lads," he said in a very strong Welsh accent. "I could not help over hearing you were English. Are you going to the town hall this morning?"

Dunkirk Town Hall,
a very grand building.

"We are indeed," Peter replied, and we were soon introduced to Michael. who was interested in this morning's service, but more keen to go to Wormhout. He asked if there would be room on the coaches. I told him that it was unlikely, as they appeared to be over-booked.

"I will go back to my hotel and bring the car so I can follow the coaches to the different sites," he said. "I have not a clue how to get there so I will follow them."

"That sounds a good plan," we replied.

"It is supposed to be two people per boat, but last time we were not checked in, so could try you luck with the town hall," I suggested. With that he said he would see us later and walked away. We drank up and walked across the square passing many veteran cars and lorries of the 1940s parked on show, with the enthusiasts all dressed in full forties uniform. It was quite a sight. At the town hall entrance, you are met with a grand double staircase. I was awestruck by a glorious stained glass window that runs between them up to the ceiling and dominates a whole wall. It depicts Dunkirk in the Middle Ages when it was a prosperous port with ships and merchants going about their business.

Many "Little Ship" people were already gathered inside, including a good number of "Free-French," the men and women who fought against the German occupation of France and members of resistance groups, displaying medals and standards, all with a confident air and a great deal of pride. Many elderly people were sitting on the windowsills and as the hall filled I was pushed back almost in the lap of one of these old ladies. I offered her my place so she could see but she declined, so I offered her my lap to sit on, and with a very big smile, she again declined.

Paul standing with the commemorative plaque, in front of that wonderful stained glass window inside the town hall.

She then chatted with her friend who looked at me and laughed. It made her day, I think! The hall was soon full, as reporters and television surrounded the small platform that was to be the focal point. Our host, the Mayor of Dunkirk took to the podium. He was introduced in English and French and gave one of the most passionate of speeches I've ever heard.

Whatever he said, boy, did he put some feeling into it. When at last he took breath, an interpreter gave us the English version, which was so bland by comparison. A small voice from behind quietly said: "That's not what he said." I spun round to see who would dare to criticise, to be confronted by a sea of smiling Frenchmen. I could do no more than smile back. They were indeed the Free French. Our commodore gave a very good reply but the speeches were soon over and wine on offer, and as we made our way to the table I noticed our Welsh man had got in. We collected a very nice plaque to commemorate the 70th anniversary of the evacuation of Dunkirk. One can only wonder what the men on the beaches would have thought if they knew we would commemorate a successful retreat 70 years in the future. I had my picture taken with the plaque in front of the stained glass window and thank goodness the window was there to improve the shot.

After lunch, we made our way to the congested square to meet the coaches and were surprised by the large police presence of cars and motorbikes. As we queued for a coach, a very big bald man, 6 foot 3 inches tall and built like a brick outhouse, wearing dark glasses and a white suit came into view. It was Michael.

"Hi lads, I brought the car. Would you like to ride with me?"

We rounded the lead coach to see an Audi Cabriolet, not very old and probably top of the range, standing amongst the coaches.

I was about to ask where was his car when he pointed to the Audi: "That's mine."

I grabbed John, who was just about to board the coaches. "Come with me," I said. The smile on Peter's face was a picture. "I don't believe this," he said, looking back at the poor people sat in a hot coach. As the coaches started to pull out, Michael slipped between them and we were off. We had a police escort and motorcycle outriders with us.

It got even better. We went through red lights and all traffic had to give way. Anyone trying to push in was kicked or sworn at. We were soon at the cemetery where the British memorial stood, but as we went to drive in the police directed us away from the parking area and were sending us back in to town. John said: "I will handle this." In his best French accent, but akin to someone from the comedy show 'Allo-'Allo, he said: "Môn sure we are with the "Little Ships", the "Little Ships"."

It was another miracle, as the police seemed to understand him and gave us our own parking space. "No problem, see," said John.

The day was very hot now and our black blazers were attracting the sun's rays. It was the best weather we were to have on the whole trip. We joined the sombre crowds and made our way toward the memorial. There were hundreds of British and French veterans and a few of us guys from the "Little Ships". The standards of many different groups lined the main path and many French civilians made up a very big crowd. The memorial was like a small temple or folly that one would encounter on an English country estate but a little more modern. A choir of local school children sung in front of the memorial in English for us. There were many representative faiths giving thanks for the sacrifice that so many gave, it was very moving. As the service concluded Peter gave me a nudge.

"Look up there, behind the choir."

In silhouette you could see Cameron taking a picture of the cut glass window in the back of the memorial; we both went for our cameras and took pictures of him. We did not know and we could not see what he was taking pictures of until we looked at our own pictures. The window was a picture of the evacuation from the beaches and Mole, with soldiers wading in the water, boats coming and going, planes fighting in the sky and bombing the troops and ships. It was a truly marvellous picture and we would never have seen it if it had not been for our roving reporter. A comical moment that turned into awe and wonder.

I have a prickly feeling on the back of my neck even writing about it.

Above: A French veteran organising visitors around the new Memorial of Hands, which symbolises the reaching out in peace, at Wormhout, the site of a WWII massacre of hundreds of Allied soldiers.

Below: Cameron (in black jacket) photographing the etched memorial window commemorating the evacuation, in a Dunkirk cemetery.

We were herded back to our transport and soon set off again with our police escort, driving quite fast through the villages and lanes. We started to notice something very strange: people were waving to us in the car! They must have taken one look at Michael and took him to be a bodyguard and us celebrities, I suppose. Peter said: "What do we do?"

I replied: "We are English, we wave back."

At Wormhout, the very small roads turned into farm tracks and eventually we parked and walked further into the countryside. The fields around us were well tended and the sugar beet was in perfect rows with no weeds or infestation of any kind. We walked up another farm track towards a little shed, which had been rebuilt but this was the site of a cattle shed where over a hundred soldiers had been murdered by the SS. On entering the atmosphere was very heavy, and looking around and reading the story of events displayed on the walls was difficult. The emotion in the building was a physical presence, wet eyes and a very heavy lump in my throat made conversation for me impossible. I wanted to run away, but I had to read all what was on display. How could anyone have survived?

It was exactly 70 years ago that it had happened, to the minute. I walked away in silence as did many others. I find even recounting this hard. There was some music and fine words and a high earth mound had been built to commemorate the site. I saw some old soldiers smiling and even laughing. Others with small tears in their eyes, gripping their sticks with white knuckles, holding their heads up but with difficulty. These old boys had seen some of this and were still here and had come back to give thanks or say goodbye, or see you again soon. I don't know, but it was the most moving of experiences I have ever witnessed and been a part of. A new monument was unveiled, of hands coming together. But all I could see in it was the image of a drowning person. It was all very emotional.

As I walked around the outside of the arena, there were hedges and trees but I was still stunned by the silence. I didn't see a single bird. And then at last, a skylark called out from an adjacent field and it gave me a very good reassuring feeling. That song was so good.

We were among the first to leave the car park and at last finding a fast road Michael put his foot down and it blew the sadness out of us as we recollected the afternoon's events. We soon arrived back at the quay side and headed to our favourite bar. Michael bid his farewells. He runs a pub in Cardiff, so if you're ever down his way you will not fail to recognise him, a very nice man.

After a couple of beers we were off to get cleaned up. Waiting for us in the lobby of the Best Hotel tonight was a statuette of Marilyn Munroe. She looked so lonely lifting her skirt round the corner of the stairs. We spent another night on the tiles in Dunkirk, another memorable meal. When I am away and eating out I like to try different foods or dishes that my wife would not give me at home, and tonight would not be any different. I ordered frogs legs cooked in butter and garlic. Poor Peter could not believe it, bless him.

He ordered salad and steamed cod. When my dinner arrived I was gob-smacked at the size of the legs. If one of these had jumped into my pond I would loose half of the water - they were huge. And meaty, that's for sure, the flesh was of good texture and firm. But I could only taste the garlic and butter, the meat itself was like chicken only tasteless. Oh well, tried it, and won't bother again. Meanwhile the banter flowed, as did the wine and beer. Trevor reiterated the fact he did not drink. We were all relieved at his statement because if he did drink, none of us would have been able to keep up with him so just a few sips by him was fine by us.

It was a cloudy morning the next day and a chilly wind was blowing straight into our room, as the window still did not shut. At breakfast, we told our TV lady Becky (we knew her name by now), that she had a berth on *Chumly* for the wreath laying ceremony later on in the day. We were going to take the cameraman Greg, so he could film her and the boat for the local news interest slot on Central TV. "Oh cool!" she said.

In no time we were back down on the quay side. The weather did not look good and we were dressed again for the winter. What with the banter from the *Ferry Nymph* brigade and our extra passenger, an officer from *HMS Monmouth,* time flew. We were soon on our way out of the lock to the sea. We passed the end of the Mole and turned to go along parallel to the beaches, following a set of markers to form a diamond shape. We were told the weather was not good enough for the fly past of the Hurricane and only the Navy helicopter would be flying. Dark clouds loomed, but fortunately the wind was coming off the land so it would not get that rough. Yet we were being led around and around in front of the beaches and for us on an open boat it was becoming unpleasant. What we did not know was that one of the French veterans had passed away as the service got under way on the shore and that is why things were taking so long. Eventually, we were allowed to break from the circuit and lay our wreaths. We moved into the middle of the circle and I stopped the engine. You would have to be a very hard man to say that this small act did not move you.

Trevor and Graham laying the wreaths.

Wreaths laid in honour of the courage, valour, self sacrifice, commitment, ingenuity, and professionalism of all those who lost their lives in the evacuation of Dunkirk, May 1940.

Peter said a few words and Trevor and Graham laid the wreaths. We had our own private thoughts and words to say inside as we laid the flower emblems in silence. The *Endeavour* gently rolling about, as if nodding approval of our actions, it was very miserable and considering what we had just done the sky matched our mood: grey.

We attended a few more events and were held back a day by bad weather but finally the flotilla was on its way back home across the Channel. But not without events: one boat broke down, another fouled its propeller and a crewman managed to cut himself while trying to free it. The lifeboats were doing what they do best, tidying up. A few porpoises and dolphins joined us, but for us it was a quiet crossing. On returning to Ramsgate, several hundred people were there to welcome us back, but early the next morning when we left the port town, there were no onlookers, all was quiet. The main event was over and we were on the last stretch, the final leg homeward bound. With a good flood tide helping us we made good time and five hours later we were going up Leigh creek. Our families were there to meet us and after what was an amazing week. *Endeavour* was back on her mooring safe and sound, the 70th anniversary was over. God willing, we will do it again for the 75th and 80th. After that I will be getting old, but the boat will be there, I am sure, and so will many of the others it is called the Dunkirk Spirit.

Reflecting on a trip like that, many thoughts go through your mind. What must it have been like taking a little boat to war? How do you cope with the disasters and death that surrounded you? Would we, or could we even, do anything like it again? How did Ramsgate cope with all the soldiers that were landed there? The townspeople fed them, gave them cigarettes and moved them all over the country. How did one telephone line at the command centre at Dover handle all the traffic? I could ask so many more questions, but we must be grateful that they all did. I have heard many stories and read many more that have brought me to tears, of valour, self sacrifice, commitment, ingenuity, professionalism and horror. Every time you speak to someone another story comes to life. We, or rather I, got a great deal of enjoyment out of this trip. We had our own camaraderie, and the moving trip to Wormhout is something I will never forget.

Unfortunately this kind of atrocity still continues to this day in some country or another, so we have not learnt from the past. I felt humbled on many occasions as I heard another Dunkirk story unfolded. What I have experienced and learnt is that there are many fine and good people in this world, but some times it takes a major event to get them moving. Dunkirk was one of those events.

Six Boats

Six boats left Leigh old town
Not knowing where they were bound
Cockle boats one and all
They had answered the nation's call

The British army was trapped in France
Trying to stop the German advance
They had been beaten back to the beach
Leaving the Navy out of reach

After several days of evacuation
More was needed, some drastic action
From river and creek around the coast
It was little ships they needed most

Ferries, fishers and pleasure craft
Anything with little draught
Our cockle boats met this criteria
In shallow water they were superior

Six Boats

To the beaches they did go
Ferrying soldiers to and fro
They were manned by all and sundry
Possibly back in the office by Monday

Organised chaos we are told
Many stories would leave us cold
But one we will tell again and again
Despite the loss and the pain

One of ours, the little Renown
Did not come back to the old town
A mine we are told was her demise
She was only small, vaporised

We must never forget what they gave
For them there is no grave
Remember them and the others too
They saved our army for me and you

An aircraft wheel and engine part hauled from the Thames Estuary seabed.

New Bones

As I have said many times, you never know what a day's fishing will bring. This day was no different. It was late August and we were fishing on the east end of the Nore Sands, which is the north side of the deep water off the Estuary in the Medway Channel. The Thames and the Medway merge here to run out to the North Sea and it is a feeding station for Dover sole before they leave for the winter. The seabed is very diverse here with patches of sand and mud. It is the mud I was looking for, the thick and black and often very smelly kind, as this is the ideal home for rag worm, which is sole's favourite food. Because of its position within the Thames and the importance of trade this area, it is a very busy place and has been since man went afloat. We have also had numerous wars and conflicts within the Thames, making it a hot spot.

Over the years, this site has provided our family with many challenges. We have caught a large number of objects here as well as much fish: bombs and shell cases are particularly commonplace. But we've also hauled cut-glass ornaments, a piano, a toilet, wash basin, shot guns, knives, pots and bottles. Some of these objects are hundreds of years old and I've handed several of them over to Southend Museum, where they are on display. One such example was a small ceramic hip flask, which was the same as one found at an East London-based pirate's house that had been excavated. We've hauled much bigger objects also, including concrete sinkers, anchors, aircraft wheels and propellers. We even once caught a whole aircraft in our nets. It was a Boulton Paul Defender - a two-seater night fighter that apparently was a useless design. That is why it was here. It was probably one that had been shot down by our own war ships, anchored in the Nore, and then used as a shooting practice target for the Navy, until someone gave it too much lead.

On this particular day, we had already caught four stone of sole and a nice four inch brass shell case. There is a lot of tide here so you only tow into it. Therefore, I went back to where we had shot the first time and shot up again, just clear of the previous tow. When we hauled second time round, it was not quite so good, but there was something caught in the middle net and it would not shake out. Vince, my crew that day, was not impressed. He was busy on deck picking up the catch, and as I shook the net vigorously, he was being covered in mud and rubbish.

"Do you have to?" he asked. With that something fell to the deck.

"Ah!" I said.

"Now what?" he asked.

"It's a bone," I replied.

"We catch loads of bones," was Vince's reply.

"But this one is human. A pelvis bone and it's a man's."

"Oh yeah, how do you know that?"

"Look at the size and shape, did you not learn anything at school?"

"No, I used to bunk off science - it was boring. I would go fishing down the pier," he said, adding: "Chuck it back. It will only be trouble."

I thought about what he said. "No, it is not that old. Someone is waiting for this person to come home," I said and put it in a box, before returning to he wheelhouse to get back down the tow. I picked up the handset to the VHF radio and called the Coastguard. I told them who I was and needed to talk to someone on the phone. Could they ring me? No problem. Seconds later my mobile rang.

"Yes Paul, Coastguard here, what can we do for you?"

That's good, I thought, at least it's someone who knows me.

"I have a question for you. I have a bone and I believe it to be a human pelvis. I do not think it has been in the water that long. Should I throw it back or shall I bring it home?"

"Wait one," was the reply. I bet they don't get questions like that very often, I thought. "We are contacting the police to get some advice, we will ring you back."

It seemed like hours but the police probably rang straight back. "Save it, give us an estimated time of arrival at your landing destination and a police car will be there to meet you."

"Thank you," I said. "We'll return on high tide at Bell Wharf."

That would be about 2.30 in the morning, a long time from now. We continued fishing, not giving the bone any further thought. The fishing was steady, but no fireworks. The good news was they were a very good sample and would I hoped to make good money. We stopped work about midnight and headed for home. At 2.15 am, we bumped alongside the quay.

"No bloody car here yet!" said Vince.

"Give them time, we are early" I replied. We loaded up the van and still no car. I rang the contact number I had been given. They knew nothing about it, but would send a car down. We waited for another half an hour, and still no one came. As I rang again, Vince said he was off and took the fish to the yard, leaving me to wait.

"Sorry, I don't know what you are talking about," said the person who answered. Was this a joke?

"Okay," I said. "I will take it up to Leigh police station and hang it on the front door."

"You can't do that," was the reply.

"Oh I think I can," I answered.

I had put the bone in a carrier bag and got in my car to take it up to the police station. When I arrived there was no one there. I hung on for a few minutes but no one came. Okay, I thought, hang it on the door, and just as I walked to the door a car turned up. A young lady constable got out the passenger side.

"Mr Gilson?"

"Yes that's me," I said, and as she walked closer I offered her the bag.

"What am I to do with that?" she asked.

I could not resist. "Take a large saucepan, half fill with water add carrots, onions, the bone and season to taste."

"You're sick," came her reply. But I could see the driver, an older man, was laughing.

"No, just tired. I am off to bed goodnight." As I drove away, I could still hear that driver chuckling away. I thought that would be that.

Some months later I found myself in North Shields, Northumbria, looking at a replacement winch for my boat. My mobile rang and a lady was on the other end.

"Hello, is that Mister Gilson? I am a sergeant in the Kent Police. I wondered if we could do an interview."

"What's it about?" I asked.

"The bone you caught, it is part of an ongoing investigation."

"Are you pulling my leg, who is this?"

"Mr Gilson, I am serious."

"Well okay." I explained and we made a date and time to meet.

A week later, a police sergeant arrived at my yard. We had a cup of tea and she told me of her search for a missing man in Kent and how she had found nothing. She had started to look further a field and came upon the bone I'd found when she had started looking in Essex. She could not tell me that much, but they had been able to identify the man through reconstructed DNA. I was asked where and when we had caught it and very little else. She thanked me profusely and said that I would probably be hearing from them again. Time passed and sure enough a letter came though the post, instructing me to attend Maidstone Crown Court to give evidence in a murder trial. I dutifully turned up on a lovely day - sunny and no wind - which was just my luck, as it would have been a great day for fishing. I checked in and was sent to a small room that had no windows. The lack of windows was not a problem, but when I looked around the room, it was nearly full of what I can only describe as the dregs of society. Women and children who either by wish or circumstance had got nowhere in life. One heavily pregnant young women was berating her partner about her condition, but was pleased she would be getting a council house. Another was saying how her partner was illegitimate and hoped he got his just deserts, because he was always beating her up. The kids were fighting and I was feeling very depressed by the whole situation. I was beginning to think Vince was right about saving the bone and all the trouble it would cause.

After what seemed an age, I was collected and taken to a very quiet hall where I was asked to sit and await a call. It was heaven by comparison. A police officer came and spoke to me about what was about to take place and what I would have to do. A very tall and well-dressed man made his way to where I was sitting, but he was pulled away by who I later learned was the prosecuting brief. The brief chatted to him for a few minutes and then came and spoke to me. He introduced himself and the tall well-dressed man.

"Would you mind, Mr Gilson, if -------- comes in first, he is the pathologist and is identifying the bone you caught? He needs to get away."

"No problem at all," I replied. The brief left us and we sat down and chatted about the bone. He asked me how and when we caught it. I asked him how they had identified it. I realised I was calling him Sir, not like me at all but he did seem a bit special. He had charisma, confidence and a manner that was a job to understand or describe. He told me he was very busy at the moment and had a great deal to do when he got back to work. As he was called into the court to give his evidence, another person came and sat with me. A young women whom I later found out was an expert with shoes and trainers. She asked if I knew who that man was. "Not a clue," I replied.

"He is the pathologist who is putting all the bodies back together after the Tube and bus bombs at Tavistock Square." She was referring to the event we now know as "7/7".

"Blimey, all he said to me was he was a bit busy."

"That," she said, "is an understatement."

We talked a bit about shoes and she asked about fishing until my name was called. I was soon in the witness box and being asked: "Do you solemnly swear to tell the truth the whole truth and nothing but the truth?" With my hand on the Bible I replied: "I will."

The jurors were sitting opposite, with the judge to my left and the defendants to my right behind their briefs. When I look toward them, I could only think that they looked like a couple of characters from Eastenders in their new suits. The judge thanked me for saving the bone and tried to relax me, I thought, with some simple questions. This was actually far from the truth, the questions were very important to the case, but I did not realise that until later. He asked me about how long I had and my family had been fishing. I replied only about 200 years, Sir. Chuckles all round.

"Mr Gilson, have you ever caught mackerel in Sheerness Harbour?"

"Well, Sir," I began, thinking it an odd question, "I did try with my father about 40 years ago. We shot a trawl and went round and round on a show of birds, but we caught nothing."

Everyone laughed! What had I said that was funny?

"In your professional opinion would you go mackerel fishing in or around Sheerness Harbour."

"No, Sir."

"Why not?"

"Well Sir, for catching mackerel the water has to be clear and around Sheerness the water is always thick or muddy. If you are using hooks, the fish have to see the feathers and then they snatch at them and bingo!" Laughter all round.

"Mr Gilson, if you were looking at a map of the sea and you saw a WK on that map, what would that mean?"

"Well Sir, it's called a chart and that would be a wreck."

"Are there many wrecks local to Sheerness Harbour?" the judge asked.

"Yes Sir, a great many ships and planes have been lost here through war or shipwreck"

"Mr Gilson, is there any well known wreck in the area?"

"Yes Sir, the *Richard Montgomery*."

"Do you know this wreck?"

"Yes Sir, she dragged her anchor and got ashore. She broke her back, near the end of the war."

"Is there anything special about this ship?"

"Well Sir, several of her holds still have explosives on board and the rumour is always that if it blows up half of Sheerness will disappear."

More chuckles.

"Have you been close to her, could you get on her?"

"Yes Sir, there are a number of buoys that tell you to keep clear, but on one occasion when I was still in the lifeboat service, we were tasked to go to her and remove someone having a picnic on her wheelhouse. He was on the roof sat in a machine-gun turret, eating cheese sandwiches." More laughter. Then there was a question from one of the defence briefs; I can not remember what was said, but everybody laughed. "Thank you, Mr Gilson, that will be all." I acknowledged the judge and left the room.

I was met by the officer who had contacted me originally. She went on to explain what had happened and why the questions had been asked. The defendants had, they believed, beaten up the victim and left him unconscious. There had been a disagreement over drugs, the police thought. The accused had left him and went somewhere else but came back some time later to find him recovering. They attacked him again and probably killed him. They took the body down to Queenborough, on the Isle of Sheppey, and put it aboard a small cabin boat. The police believe the body had been wrapped in chicken wire and made fast to an anchor. They took this boat, probably without permission, and went to the wreck of the *Richard Montgomery*. They had claimed that they were going fishing for mackerel. It was thought that they dumped the body into the wreck, and were probably very surprised when a body part turned up. She stopped talking as two women came over to me. It was the sister and I think the wife of the deceased. The sister clutched my hand and thanked me so much for bothering to save the bone. They could now grieve and move on. They were so very pleased that it was nearly all over. Those few moments made all the hassle worthwhile, as I had thought right from the start, someone was waiting for him to come home.

The accused were found guilty on three charges, but not of murder.

Spooky Stuff

O VER THE YEARS there have been many very odd things happen while we have worked my current boat , the *Janeen*. You can judge them for yourself.

The first time I encountered something odd was while working in Leigh on the engine; a water pump had worn out and myself and Peter Lilly, my engineer, we were replacing it. We had stripped down the pump, removed the worn out parts and it was ready to be reassembled, so we stopped to have a cup of tea at the café on the other wharf. After only a short break, we were back at work, but things weren't right. A small club hammer was not where we had left it. After some searching, we found it on a cross beam at the front of the engine room but we had not been that end of the engine room. The new gasket for the pump had disappeared completely. We searched the whole engine room but never found it. Peter had to make a new one. We never solved that mystery.

Another time, we were fishing and hauling, when a voice said: "Jump." This was an order. I jumped just as the block failed, probably caused by a pin coming loose, releasing the wire which flew across the deck where I had been standing. Tim, my crew at the time, just looked at me in shock. If I had not jumped, I would have been severely injured.

When we rest, we use the *Janeen*'s ample cabin and wake each other up with a coded tap on the cabin ladder. This is part of the ship and it resonates into the cabin. "Tap, tap tap tap, tap," is how it goes, quite simple and it works well. But the tapping began taking place on its own. We would be asleep and the tapping would start, so you got dressed and went up to the wheelhouse to find that whoever was steering had not called. We put it down to our imagination, but then it happened several times when we were still awake.

It got so bad that I started shouting at the noise: "Stop mucking about, we need some rest." It did indeed slow up and oddly got quieter.

When you are at the helm of *Janeen*, you are listening to the engine all the time, waiting for her to start to labour or even miss a beat with a dirty filter. You can feel the movement of the boat and sense the gear going over the seabed. One particular day, the engine room door opened and then closed all by itself. I heard it quite clearly. I looked down the companion way to see the door shut, only to sit down and hear it open again. Tim was on deck so it was not him, so I went down to check why it was opening and closing on its own. I opened the door to find that a water pipe had split and salt water was spraying all over the engine room. Over the years, this has happened many times, and we have had hydraulic pipes go or injectors fail and even a leak that threatened to sink the boat. There is nothing wrong with the door or its catch, but it opens and closes on its own. We have learnt that whatever happens, if that door opens, you go down and check.

Only recently, I started the engine up ready to go to sea and as I went to close the door it pulled back not letting me close it. I opened it again, looked inside, checked and tried to close it again and it again pulled back. Now a logical explanation must be found, I told myself. But then I saw that one of the bolts had come out of the companion way ladder and if I had put weight on it, the ladder would have come off with me falling backwards. I replaced the bolts and checked the door again and it closed in its natural manner.

When my youngest daughter, Julia, came to work with us with one of her friends - they were about 11 at the time and knew nothing of our spooky resident. They went down into the cabin and went to sleep while we steamed to the fishing grounds. Once home, they told Heather when they were trying to sleep in the bunks, they felt someone kept blowing in their faces.

Then one night, when I was at home the phone rang about 2am.

"Paul, the *Janeen*'s on fire, the brigade is on it way."

I was down to the quay in no time. The fire brigade was already there, but puzzled. There was no fire; there had been several reports and calls to them but on arrival they found no fire. Using a heat seeking camera, they had made their way down to the cabin and found a strong heat source in the cabin fire -it was showing that it was indeed very hot. Now comes the puzzle: the fire was sat on the cabin table was totally disconnected from fuel and exhaust pipe as we were changing a bearing on the shaft below where the fire would normally sit. I explained that some very strange things happened on this boat and the officers knew exactly what I meant.

The next morning, we found the cause of the fire: some yob had pulled the smoke float (a distress signal) off the side of the wheelhouse and it had drenched the boat in red smoke so she looked on fire. This did not account, however, for the heat in the fire in the cabin, as the machine said it was very hot yet it was cold to the touch. On another occasion, we were working on deck and I came back into the wheelhouse to find a ring on the gas cooker was alight. I was a bit surprised as it was not the ring that we used to make the tea or cooked on. I asked Andy if he had lit it. He denied all knowledge of lighting it and why should he, he asked. I had come to the conclusion that what ever we had on the boat was not harmful but was good and had I felt a sense of humour.

At a recent industry meeting, I met someone from where the *Janeen* was built. I was asking him about the *Janeen* and her history as we had had many problems with the Maritime and Coastguard Agency (MCA) about stability and the like. (We had later found out that the MCA had two boats called *Janeen* in the same folder and this caused 15 years of confusion!) However, he misheard me and replied that she caught plenty of fish and was a good earner but had a job retaining crew.

"What was the problem then?"

He stared into my eyes and said:"You know, don't you?"

"I know that there is something there, but it not a problem."

"Well it scared the crap out of our people that's for sure," he added, before quickly making his excuses and moving away.

Whatever we have on her, I cannot explain it. You do not have to believe what I have said, but I and several others have experienced it and we even talk to it. As yet it has not spoken back, but perhaps it will one day.

As for the gasket, we have had a new engine and had the whole of the engine room cleaned out. We looked in every place it could have gone and places where it could not. As to this day we have not found it, but that is not to say it may not turn up one day.

Above: Dad's boat, the Paul Peter, passing Southend Pier in a local trawler race.

Below: The Anja and Janeen leaving Southend Pier to sprinkle Dad's and his son Peter's ashes on his favourite fishing grounds.

Southend Pier on Fire, Again

I HAVE BEEN INVOLVED with the Southend Pier since I can remember, and I have seen it burn four times, as well as cut in half by a clapped out old tanker.

My early memories of the pier come clearly to me. I was six years old and I had to write about the pier pavilion burning down in school. I remember many of my classmates did not even know that the pier had been on fire when our teacher told us to write about it. Dad had helped people off the pier with some small boats and I knew so much about it that day at school. I managed to write two lines about the event and drew a picture of the pavilion on fire. It was possibly one of my longest stories or essays I ever wrote, until now.

At that early age, the pier was already part of my life. Dad would be down at the boathouse and after Sunday school at the Salvation Army, I would walk down the high street and go to the pier train station. I would normally have one or two of my cousins with me and we would walk up to the gate and say: "Gilsons." That was good enough, the ticket collector would let us through. Most of these men had watched me grow up and Dad would tell them that I would be coming down, but it did give a small boy an immense amount of power as we would often walk past many people queuing for the trains.

It was a ritual that on Sunday mornings, the crew of the lifeboat would meet to catch the 10 o'clock train. They would clean and wash the boat and practise with the new D-boats or "rubber ducks" that were just coming into service. We had no idea then just how these boats were to revolutionise the service and have save probably thousands of lives. If we pleaded enough, or if they had time, we would get a short ride around the pier in one.

My in-laws lived in Undercliff Gardens and we had only been married a few years when we received a phone call from Harold, my father-in-law.

"Paul, the pier is on fire!"

We had only just got home after visiting him but we went back to his house and watched the pier burn. I wanted to go and help but Heather was having none of it. She quite rightly said that the duty crew would be there and what did I know about fires? The fire took place in the middle of a drought. It was 1976 and water was very short so the pier was tinder dry. Eventually two tugs came down from Gravesend and put their fire hoses on the now substantial fire. It was too little, too late.

One must be grateful that nobody was hurt but the new and modern fire pump that had been installed at the pier head never did work properly. You were lucky if you could get it to start and if you got it to pump water, that was a miracle. Yet the old out-of-date one built in a concrete bunker did work when it was tried after that fire. Those first few minutes would have been critical. By the time the fire brigade arrived, it was all too late.

Some ten years passed before we had another episode of the pier drama, in June 1986. This time it was an early evening and we were going to work. Dad and I were going after eels, and as we came out from Leigh we could see smoke and a lot of activity at the pier head. We steamed down to the pier and went alongside. A tanker, the MV Kingsabbey, had ploughed through the end of the pier and cut the lifeboat slipway in half, causing major structural damage due to the destruction of iron piles and supporting girders and left a 70-foot gap in the pier. Dad at this time was the Southend Lifeboat Hon. Sec. so he stayed behind to sort out the mess.

The lifeboat was trapped in the boathouse. There was no way it could go down the slipway, so another method had to be worked out to get her back in to the water. It was decided that she would have to go out through the side of the boathouse and somehow be lowered to the water, or mud as it was at that time. With many hands and the fire brigade, the side of the boathouse was knocked out and ropes and wires were used to hoist the boat up and out of the hole they had made. Wires had been run across to the main walkway of the pier and somehow a larger version of a bosun's chair erected. She was pulled out and lowered to the incoming tide.

This was some feat, yet I have never heard it mentioned or written about, not even a single picture. So this is my tribute to the many unsung men who worked together to get the lifeboat back in service and sought no recognition for their deeds.

But this event created a very difficult time for the station, as a temporary boathouse had to be quickly erected at Two Tree Island (it took just a few days), until eventually a new boathouse was built at the end of the pier. The old one was blown up, but it took three attempts as it was so well constructed.

The next part of the saga begins in 1995, when I was mending nets in my yard in Southend and I could smell burning.

"Can you smell that?" I asked one of my staff.

"Must be a fire," he replied, and then said: "Look!"

The sky went dark. I ran down the road and could see the roof of the bowling alley on the pier was bellowing smoke. Running back to the yard, I rang the Hon. Sec.

"The bowling alley is on fire. I am going to try and get the IRB under way before it gets too bad." I cannot remember the reply. We just ran.

The inshore boathouse was situated alongside the pier but virtually underneath it. It contained the inshore boat and all the equipment needed to operate it, plus some 30 gallons of petrol. I was on the scene quickly, as my yard is only a short distance away. Another crewman, Nick Finnegan, turned up and we got the boat in the water very fast with no gear or life jackets. We just got it under way as more crew were arriving and the boathouse was evacuated. Again with so many willing hands so much can be done and this was again the case, all the fuel and gear was moved a safe distance from the fire. By the time we had everything out of harm's way, the bowling alley was totally alight. Nick and I evacuated the visitors and staff from the pier head in the lifeboat and put them back ashore. If only we had had a camera that day. We had the pole position to take pictures of the pier yet again burning down. The colours of the flames I will never forget: the blues, greens, yellows and reds, as different metals burnt off. The temperature of the fire was truly amazing. You could feel the heat on your face from nearly a quarter of a mile away. If hell is like this, it may be hot, but also has a certain beauty to it.

Fortunately, the fire did not reach the boathouse but it did cut the boathouse off at the end of the pier. It was decided that a duty crew should take refuge at the pier head until communications were restored. From somewhere a bag of filled rolls turned up and five of us remained at the pier head feeling a bit cut off, watching the blaze from afar. We stayed there until it was deemed safe to go ashore. Fortunately, the walkway round the west side of the bowling alley had not been touched. Since then, the pier has endured yet another fire: in 2005, a fire destroyed the pier café, shop, train station and the The Jolly Fisherman pub and caused substantial damage to the pier superstructure. Southend Lifeboat crew were deployed to transport the first fire fighters to the scene, but again due to the low tide, pumps installed on the pier were rendered ineffective.

It took several months before a new station was built and the pier reopened, but only temporary toilets and an RNLI visitor's centre are currently open.

To make matters worse, during rebuilding work in 2011, a barge that was carrying the waste away and bringing in new materials broke its moorings and damaged the walkway, temporarily stopping access yet again. It seems every decade our much loved pier gets herself into trouble.

I am sure this will not be the last time.

You Can Rely On Ford

OVER THE YEARS I am continually reassessing my opinion of just how stupid people can be. Here are some classics from the annals of idiocy.

One memorable incident was when the Sheerness Lifeboat went to the aid of a craft bound for Southampton. The skipper had left the River Medway with a road map, no charts and the same amount of fuel as he would use if he were going by car. His theory was that if he kept the land on his right hand side he would be okay. The flaw in his plan was he had not taken in to account the Isle of Sheppey and after going around the island several times he ran out of fuel!

I have encountered several episodes of this nature over the years. Another comes to mind was not long after I was married, so I was possibly 20 and still working with Dad. We had been fishing just south of the Red Sand Towers, a WWII anti-aircraft platform based on seven towers. In the 1960s, it was home to one of many pirate radio stations that popped up around the coast. It was the second day that we had worked the area. We had seen a small yacht there the first day and he was still there the next day. He was not anchored and was just drifting about. It was calm so we did not think that much about it until the last tow when we passed quite close to him. The yacht was no more than 16 feet with a small cabin, and one man at the helm. Another man was sitting in the cabin hatch, and he waved at us as we were passing,but it was wave of come over, not hello. Dad shaped the *Anja* over in their direction and the older man shouted out.

"Have you got any water to spare?"

I looked at Dad. "When we have hauled we will come over," I shouted back. We were on the last haul so it was not a problem.

We hauled, picked up the fish, washed down, cleared the deck and got the beams aboard. We slowly went alongside. The older guy was aboard in a flash, the younger man at the helm just sat there. I took a line from their bow and made it fast.

"Would you like some water?" I asked.

"A hot cup of tea would be nice," he replied. This is not what we were expecting - we were not a café! Dad gave a nod so I went down the cabin and put the kettle on. Dad came out of the wheelhouse to talk to the old guy and went on to ask him: "So you have been here two days, where are you bound?"

"Margate."

"Margate?" Dad exclaimed, "That's miles over there."

"Well my son knows where it is. We have been following the red light, so when it's dark we will be okay."

"The red light?" Dad repeated, raising his eyebrows. "When did you come to sea?"

"We left Rochester on Sunday afternoon."

"It's Tuesday, you have only left the Medway by a few miles!"

"Yes," he said. "But we will see the red light later and we will be off again."

"But you were here yesterday?"

"My son said it was the tide that brought us back. He thinks we will be there in the morning. We were just short of water."

I had brought the tea up and gave them a cup each. The son sat motionless at the tiller, not saying a word. They had not drunk or eaten for some time in my opinion, as they could not get the tea inside them quick enough. Dad looked up. "I will tell you what, we will tow you up to Sheerness and you can get some food and water then make up your mind what you are doing."

With no argument or discussion, that is what we did. I wondered about that red light for years.

Still with Dad, we were on our way to the NW Shingles crossing the Oaze Bank, when a flash speed boat came alongside and eased down. A well dressed man came out on deck and asked: "Can you tell me the way to the Thames?"

We pointed. "That way."

A quick thank you and off he went at 25 knots or more, leaving us shrugging our shoulders.

Some years later, when working in my own boat by the Shingles Bank, which is in between the Princes and the Edinburgh's major shipping channels in the Thames, Tim, my crew spotted a boat we had seen in the same spot the previous day. I looked through the binoculars. They were not going anywhere just drifting about first going one way then the other.

"I am going to speak to them as I have seen this before. I think they are lost," I said. After we had hauled, we pulled the gear alongside and steamed over to them. "Are you okay?" I asked.

"Yeah we're fine."

"I saw you yesterday. Are you sure you're not lost?"

"We are following the Ford boat to Belgium."

"The Ford boat?"

"Yeah the blue one, with Ford written on the side. We cannot catch her but we have been following her for the last two days as she goes to Belgium."

Tim, who has no time for amateurs, was shaking his head and told them it straight. "Look, I don't know how to put this, but there are two boats that look the same and they go back and forth every day. You have been following one in then following the other out. That is why you are still here!"

A total look of disbelief was all they could give us for a few minutes. "Two? And they go each way?" they said, obviously gutted and embarrassed.

"Margate is over there," I said pointing to the land. "The tide is coming in, so you can go straight there to buy a compass and some charts maybe?"

"Thank you, we will do that." And with that they sailed off to the south and weren't there the next day.

On another day, we were in the West Swin, working the deep water of Shoe Hole. Tide was high and flowing when out of the murk came a large gin palace. We were talking £500,000 plus. It was fabulous, doing 30 knots at least. He came right alongside not quite touching the side of the boat. A big man came out on deck wearing a black shirt and so much gold, that if he had fallen over the side he would have drowned.

"Hi lads, I'm having a bit of trouble getting to London. I left Bradwell yesterday and have found a few sand banks. Am I going the right way now?"

We pointed and nodded. "That's the way."

"Thank you," he said, and as before he was gone.

All Tim could say was: "Did you see the patio doors on that thing? I could not afford those for my house!"

But the winning tale of stupidity must be about the cocklers from Kings Lynn. I was not involved but as stupidity goes this is a classic. It went something like this. Norwich City were playing away at Southend United.

At that time, we had a visiting cockle fleet based in Brightlingsea. They had come from ports around the Wash. Two young crewmen, being keen football supporters, had got their hands on a small motor boat and had set off for Southend by sea to catch the game. This is not actually that far when the tide is in, but half way across the Maplin Sands they had run out of fuel. The Southend Lifeboat was dispatched to pick them up and towed them to Southend. They were too late for the game so they bought some more fuel and set off back to Brightlingsea. They made it over the Maplins only to run out of fuel again when they reached the Buxy Sands. This time, the West Mersea Lifeboat towed them in. They had only bought the same amount of fuel that they had bought for the outward trip!

Runner up for the stupidity title is as follows. I was on Sunday lifeboat duty and we were cooking our dinner in the boathouse, which is a bit of a ritual. The weekend duties could be boring so to spice the day up we would take turns cooking a dinner. It could be a curry or roast, partridge on red cabbage with juniper berries (a personal favourite), a chilli, or steaks. You name it, we cooked it. On the whole, we lived very well. We washed our feast down with a glass of beer then settled in to watch a game of football or the Grand Prix on the telly. We had already exercised the lifeboat earlier that morning so we were in relaxed mode.

A call came through from the Coastguard: "A small cabin boat going round and round near the West Leigh middle buoy, no sign of life."

We were soon in the water and on our way, it was only a few minutes before we saw this 20ft cabin cruiser going round and round. I matched the circle she was making and called out: "Any one at home?" Nothing.

"Okay, I will put you aboard," I said to Giles, who is a big lad with what I would call a lovely turn of phrase. I put the bow of the lifeboat gently alongside and Giles hopped aboard. He looked in the wheelhouse window and turned and smiled that turned into a huge grin. "You're going to like this!"

I looked back. "Trust me you will" he laughed. With that a a naked man appeared. He crawled out the wheelhouse door, while holding up a pair of trousers to cover himself. Behind him was a dishevelled young woman, covering herself with a black plastic bag.

"Ever so sorry," he said. "We hit a wave and knocked over the sugar and I have been sweeping it up. It took longer than I thought."

As we left them one of the crew said: "And don't call me sugar."

We were still laughing and grinning as we put the boat away.

Passing the sugar and sweeping up took on a whole new meaning in the boathouse.

The Birds and Bees

I HAVE A GREAT love and appreciation for nature and am constantly blown away by the beauty of the Thames Estuary and the wildlife living here. I am also astounded at the audacity of some of these creatures.

I have had so many encounters with nature, with birds and mammals, too many to mention, so here are some of the most memorable. My earliest thoughts go back to when I was very small and we were carted off to see a circus. It was a day out for the whole family, so it was with a multitude of aunts, uncles, grandparents, friends and neighbours that we filled a coach. As I remember, it was all to do with a sea lion called Fritzy, who had escaped from a boat carrying him across the Thames in London. Once overboard, he would not come back to his trainer. He was enjoying his freedom and after many failed attempts to recapture him, calls were made to the Ministry of Fisheries to see if they could help. The call eventually ended up at Gilsons Fishermen of Southend. My grandparents at first thought the call was a hoax but they were eventually convinced it was genuine. A lorry was loaded with nets, a dinghy and anything they felt may be useful in capturing a seal alive. After some time, the seal was captured safe and sound by the Gilsons. The reward was two new clinker-built dinghies (which at that time was the latest design of boat - built with overlapping planks to form a water-tight seal) and a family trip to the circus, plus of course a huge amount of publicity for Billy Smart's Circus!

Not long after this Dad brought home a seal pup, probably a grey seal. It had been found in a small pond in Chalkwell Park - presumably someone had felt it could live in there. At this time, there was a small zoo in the park and this would have been no doubt an added attraction. Unfortunately it would not feed so Dad took it back to sea.

It may have been weak, I don't know, but Dad told me he cradled it in his arms and when he let it go, it swam away looking at him and crying. It upset my dad just relating the story. Around this same time, Dad came home with a story about a huge parrot that the seagulls had forced down and how he tried to save it, but the gulls killed it before he could get alongside it.

My first personal experience with the Estuary's natural world was when a racing pigeon flew into the wheelhouse of Dad's boat, the *Paul David*. We gave it some water and it stayed with us all day. To be fair to the pigeon, the wheelhouse could have been mistaken for a pigeon loft. It did not leave until we were nearly back at Southend, and this has happened many times since.

I first saw my first colony of seals on the Estuary while out fishing as a boy with Dad. They were resting on the West Barrows sandbanks as they have done for possibly thousands of years. Whenever Dad picked up the dip bucket and hit it with a hammer, the seals looked up and wobbled their way into the water before popping up near the boat and staring at us. That interaction has happened many times with seals and I am sure they enjoy people spotting.

Not that long ago, five or six seals began resting on the sandbank next to my mooring in the Ray. This was quite a new thing, as for years we hadn't seen a single one. On this particular day, we had just returned to our mooring at low tide from a night of work. The creek was dry so we loaded the motorboat and waited for the tide to return. As we waited, the seals were taking a great interest in us swimming around, looking and taking stock of what we were doing. As we left the *Janeen* and headed up the creek, one seal followed us into the shallow water. It went past us and back looking at us now and again. My crew at the time was Andy. He had been my Dad's crew and had taken over when Tim started working ashore to sort the extra fish that we had started to handle.

"That seal is showing off, it's giving us a show of how good he is," I said. With that, the seal went past us like a torpedo. He was only just under the water as it was so shallow. It was just not what one would expect from a wild animal. Andy passed me a couple of small whiting, which I threw into the water near the seal and he appeared to take them. But as we started to touch the ground, the seal was not so keen to come into such a shallow and narrow environment. We chatted about how marvellous the seal was and how very well adapted it was to its world. When we returned the next morning, it was very peaceful, a calm and warm day, and the seals were there again, with one more inquisitive than the rest, coming close to us as we loaded up the boat.

We were prepared this time as we had saved some pouting to feed the seals. We left *Janeen* a little later on the tide. There was more water in the creek than the day before, and as we left on the motorboat, this one animal followed us at a safe distance. We threw him a couple of fish and he followed us most of the way in and had an easy meal for his troubles. The next day we had saved it some fish, but we were in a bit of a rush and did not think about feeding it until we were well under way and in the creek.

"I wonder," I said to Andy, as I held up a fish. I waved it about crying out: "Come and get it, fishy, fishy."

Andy called into doubt my sanity and finished with: "You must be joking!"

I will never forget the sight of this seal torpedoing like a porpoise toward us. As it got close, I threw the fish in front of it, only to see it catch it. I took another fish and this time I held it up, again calling out: "Fishy, fishy, here fishy." With that he came straight towards me and swam alongside. I gave it another fish and he dropped behind. I again held out another fish as we went along, and he came even faster this time, right alongside and swam next to the boat.

I then did something one only dreams about. I held the fish out at arm's length. The seal lifted itself high out of the water and I dropped the fish into its mouth, just a couple of inches away from my hand. It is a job to describe the feeling of euphoria I felt as the seal swam away. But I learnt two things: despite the smiley face, a seal has a mouth full of teeth and its breath stinks of rotting fish!

Andy and I went home with smiles on our faces that nothing could wipe off. I told my kids all about it. But I am sure it did not sink in with those I told, just how fantastic it was to feed a wild animal like that. It brings a smile to my face even now as I write. How many people have done that, I wonder?

Being at sea, I often sit and watch the birds that fly about a fishing boat. They are mostly gulls and terns inshore, but also fulmars and the odd kittiwake offshore, not forgetting the regal gannet. We take herring gulls or black-back gulls for granted, but when we work off the coast of Suffolk, near Aldeburgh, we encounter a very clever sort of bird. The birds here know when we are working or just towing. I think they have figured out that when we wear oilskins there will be food about, as when we are dressed in ordinary clothes they leave us alone. I have put this theory to the test many times. We have got to the grounds and shot and not seen a bird, nothing on the sea, and sky is also empty. Yet as soon as we start to haul, the sky fills up with hundreds of them as if by magic. They are very brave here. As we pick up the catch, they walk around the deck just out of reach, picking up small fish and tit-bits. They have even developed a pecking order. When we start gutting, they line up along the boats rail and we can even feed them, one by one. The braver ones then creep up behind us and steal fish that we have gutted from the wash tub or even out of the baskets as they drain after washing. Then when we are done and cleaned up, the birds disappear. Only to come back and start all over again when we haul.

When fishing offshore, I enjoy watching the fulmars. We had three with us all day once, and I called them the three stooges. They would squabble and argue all the time, fighting over the small pieces of gut as we threw it overboard, giving small pecks and shoves to each other. It was good entertainment. They have learnt that they can run under the lee of the boat with their wings out, which the gulls cannot do, and fall out of the sky at great speed. They have even developed a timed flight to beat the gull to the smaller pieces of gut, as they cannot get the larger bits into what must be a very small mouth. It's just magic to watch. Many years ago, we were fishing for cod near the Red Sand Towers. It was just getting light and I was making a cup of tea, when from the wheelhouse window I spotted a short-eared owl perched on a stack of fish boxes looking at me. I was watched for probably ten minutes or more. It looked at me from every angle, twisting its head from side to side. I often wondered what it was thinking or what it made of me.

One very nice summer's day, Andy and I were mending a large hole in one of our nets and the *Janeen* was making her way up river on auto pilot. We were only just in gear, moving slowly with a new flood tide to some new grounds, when I heard what I can only describe as a loud snort. As I was only looking at what I was doing, I assumed it was Andy.

"Are you okay?" I asked.

"Sorry?" he replied.

"I thought you caught you breath?"

"No, it was you!"

"Nope, not me"

With that it happened again. This time I was looking at Andy when I heard a big sigh from behind him. As I was some distance from the side of the boat, I could actually see through one of the scuppers, and there swimming alongside the boat, was a big black head of a seal. It was watching us. "You're being watched," I said to Andy. "Very slowly, turn round and look over the side." Andy turned and was greeted with a quizzical look from this large animal that was swimming sideways, only a couple of feet away. The seal was studying what Andy was doing and lifted itself up so possibly half its very big body was out of the water.

"I think you have pulled again, Andy!"

The animal swam with us for some time, watching and taking in all we were doing. Another magical moment.

On another occasion we were fishing the Long Sand head area, and every time we hauled we had sole with their heads missing. It did not take too long to work out that a seal was stealing them as we were towing. As the trip progressed, the animal became more relaxed and started taking them only when we were hauling and the gear was on the surface. He would surface some way behind the gear, then come up behind the cod ends and pull the fish through the meshes. I would assume this was an easier method for him, as the number of fish we caught without heads dropped. What made things worse, he would make a big thing of showing us the sole before he swallowed them. Seals may have a butter-would-not-melt-in-your-mouth look, but they are top predators and they learn quickly.

Just before we had this book ready to take to the printers, my crew and I had another encounter with a big bull harbour seal in the Barrow Deeps. He often see him with his distinctive black coat and white collar, which looks like he is wearing a cravat. He he reminds me of an old gentleman waiting for his dinner as he lifts himself up to look at us. This time, he started following us while we were towing and it was soon obvious that every time he surfaced he was eating a sole. He would surface, swim to just a few yards behind the boat, and then show us his dinner. When we did haul, we had several headless fish in our catch, and just to rub it in, after eating half a dozen fish, he swam on top of our middle net when it was in the surface and rolled on it, appearing to scratch himself, with what appeared great satisfaction. He was with us all that day. Entertaining he may be, clever he most certainly is.

Unfortunately, as daylight came on our next trip, there he was again with that distinctive collar - no mistake. I saw him surface some distance away, and like a homing torpedo he was just behind us. For our first haul of the day, we had done okay with two full nets, but then saw the third net didn't have a single sole in it. There must be something wrong with it, I thought. To make sure we pulled the net back on deck to check. There was nothing wrong. When we hauled the next time, it was the same again. He must have gone into the net to steal the fish and come out while we were towing. I admire him and hate him all at the same time!

Paul aboard the Janeen, enjoying a cup of tea and looking out for that seal!

In the same week, I was entertained by a large flock of gannets, over three hundred, and so many they drove the other gulls away. With their distinctive cry, like an old car horn being sounded, the gannets make their dive behind the boat for the small fish that we are obliged by law to throw back over the side. They then rest in little gangs, looking like groups of melting snowmen on a green sea, waiting for the next haul, or for my crew to start gutting the fish so they can feed again. On this same trip, a chaffinch landed on deck and had a walk around, totally unafraid of us. It just walked around us as we worked.

My world is a fantastic place and I am entertained by the natural world every day. Many birds have taken refuge on my boat but one of the most exciting was a pair of goldcrests.

Goldcrests are our smallest British bird and most springs, I see some landing on the boat as they migrate. This pair liked the area around the winch, probably interested in my many resident spiders. I was trying to get a picture of them with my phone camera, again to no avail. I sat on the wheelhouse step, hoping that one would stay still long enough for me to take its picture. When one landed on the brake handle, I thought I had it. I lifted the camera to take the picture and the bird took off, but it did not fly away. It landed on my phone and then looked into the lens of the phone camera. It must have been disappointed because it then jumped down and walked up and down my trousers as I sat there.

But I did finally get my picture!

Nothing like having a little bird making her way up your leg!